What I Believe

WHAT
I BELIEVE

Anthony Kenny

continuum
LONDON • NEW YORK

Continuum
The Tower Building, 11 York Road, London SE1 7NX
80 Maiden Lane, Suite 704, New York NY 10038

www.continuumbooks.com

Extract of 'Friday's Child' by W. H. Auden used with permission of
Faber & Faber

First published 2006

British Library Cataloguing-in-Publication Data
A catalogue record for this book is available from the British Library.

ISBN: 0–8264–8971–0 (hardback)
0–8264–9392–0 (paperback)

Typeset by Kenneth Burnley, Wirral, Cheshire
Printed and bound in Great Britain by MPG Books, Ltd, Bodmin, Cornwall

Contents

Acknowledgements

I am most grateful to Robin Baird-Smith who suggested that I should write this book, and to Ben Hayes, Anya Wilson and their colleagues at Continuum who assisted it to press. The thoughts expressed in the book are the outcome of many years of reading, listening and talking, and very many of them are due to other people. In a book of this personal nature I have dispensed with footnotes, but any reader who is interested in the genealogy of my ideas will be able to trace them to their progenitors by consulting the books listed at the end. To all from whom I have learnt I am deeply grateful. It may of course turn out, but I hope it will not, that the person to whom I owe most thanks is my friend Richard Harries, the Bishop of Oxford, who cautioned me against writing a book such as this.

Anthony Kenny
January 2006

All proofs or disproofs that we tender
Of His existence are returned
    Unopened to the sender.

W. H. Auden, 'Friday's Child'

1

The Story of My Ideas

I was born in Liverpool in 1931, the son of John Kenny and Margaret Kenny (née Jones). My mother was the second eldest of five children, of a keenly Catholic family. By the time of my birth she had lost two brothers and a sister, and her only surviving sibling was her youngest brother, Alexander Jones, then in training for the priesthood in the English College in Rome. My father was an engineer on a steamship. When he met my mother he was a lapsed Catholic and a freemason, but at her persuasion he returned to the Church and resigned from his lodge. My father and mother, however, soon discovered that they were ill suited to each other, and at a time before my earliest memories they had separated. My mother returned to her earlier career as a librarian, and I was brought up largely by my devout grandmother until her death in 1942. The place of my father – both before and after his death at sea during the Battle of the Atlantic – was taken by my Uncle Alec, whose ordination in Rome I attended as a two-year-old. Alec returned to England in 1935 to teach, for the rest of his life, at the Liverpool archdiocesan seminary at Upholland. He was best known, later in life, as the editor of the English Jerusalem Bible.

Alec was a person who, throughout his life, charmed everyone who met him, and it surprised no one when I decided that I wanted to follow in his footsteps. I was enrolled in the junior school at Upholland at the then standard age of 12, and I was educated there (principally in Latin, Greek, history and religion) until the age of 18. In 1949 I was one of two sixth-formers sent from the Liverpool archdiocese to the English College in Rome, and I remained there for eight years, following courses in philosophy and theology at the Pontifical Gregorian University.

The 'Greg' was run by Jesuits; lectures were given in Latin to audiences of hundreds, and conformed to a pattern of studies laid down in an encyclical of Pope Pius XI, *Deus Scientiarum Dominus*. Many of our Jesuit teachers were learned men, but it took quite unusual gifts, which few of them possessed, to be able to inspire students within the constraints of medium and curriculum. From 1949 to 1952 I was instructed in Thomistic philosophy – '*philosophia ad mentem Sancti Thomae*' as the Papal instructions had it – but the course involved almost no study of Aquinas's own writings, only of textbooks written by our professors. I found much of the philosophy unconvincing and repulsive, and on

vacation in England after taking my third-year licentiate I seriously considered abandoning the course and
leaving the seminary.

I did however return to Rome and persevere through
the four years' study of theology, which were indeed
more congenial than the philosophy course. One of the
professors, Maurizio Flick S. J., was capable of lecturing
in Latin as brilliantly as I have ever heard anyone
lecture in English. He took us through the teaching of
Augustine on the Creation and the Fall, on predestination, election and redemption; his vision of the narrative of salvation remained vivid in my mind long after
I ceased to accept the teaching authority of the
Church. In 1955, a year before the licentiate in
theology, I was ordained priest.

The Archbishop who ordained me, the future
Cardinal Godfrey, instructed me to return to Rome
after my licentiate for graduate studies in theology. By
this time I had become interested in the kind of philosophy being taught currently in English universities, and
I chose as my dissertation topic 'Linguistic Analysis and
the Language of Religion'. I had the good fortune to be
assigned as my supervisor at the Gregorian Fr Bernard
Lonergan S.J., who was to become well known as a
philosopher for his book *Insight*. He tried to make me
see that St Thomas should not be judged by the de-
hydrated versions of his thought in textbooks. It was
necessary to come to grips with his original massive

3

works – and Lonergan would describe to me his own decades of striving, as he put it, 'to reach up to the mind of Aquinas'.

It was not, however, until I left Rome that I really began to appreciate the philosophical genius of Aquinas. Given the topic of my dissertation, the Archbishop agreed that it would be sensible for me to spend the second year of my graduate studies in Oxford, then the world centre of analytic philosophy. There I met the Dominican Herbert McCabe and the Birmingham philosopher Peter Geach, who soon convinced me that it was possible to combine the techniques of linguistic analysis with an appreciation of the teaching of St Thomas. But the person who most influenced me in Oxford was Peter's wife, Elizabeth Anscombe, who through hours of patient, and sometimes painful, tuition brought me to realize the genius of her teacher Wittgenstein and his significance for the philosophy of our time.

After I had started work in Oxford, the archdiocesan authorities discovered that if I became a full student of the university, rather than a visitor from an overseas institution, I would qualify for a grant from my local authority, and thus relieve the Church of considerable expense. Accordingly, I was encouraged to enrol as a graduate student to write a dissertation for a second doctorate, and I began to look about for a suitable topic. On Anscombe's advice, I decided to write my thesis on the intentionality of psychological verbs. The topic was approved by the philosophy sub-faculty, and I was assigned Antony Quinton as my supervisor – the beginning of a lifelong friendship. Anscombe gave me access to appropriate unpublished papers of Wittgenstein, and Quinton was a wonderful guide to contemporary philosophical literature. I learnt much about philosophy during my two years as a resident graduate student, and I successfully completed my thesis on religious language for the Gregorian, and passed the doctorate examinations there. I never proceeded to the doctorate however, partly because I did not consider the thesis worth publishing, which was one of the conditions for the degree.

There was another reason also. Pontifical doctoral candidates had to take an oath rejecting various modern heresies. The oath included the statement that it was possible to demonstrate the existence of God. This was something of which I had become more and more doubtful; indeed during the writing of my dissertation I had become disturbed by the difficulty even of attaching meaning to statements about God, let alone establishing their truth. Initially I was over-impressed by the logical positivist demand that all meaningful statements must be capable of verification or falsification by experience; but even after I had been converted from positivism to Wittgenstein's much more subtle philosophy of language, I continued to find it difficult to attach a clear sense to many of the doctrines of the Church that as a priest I was committed to teaching.

I left Oxford with very little of my dissertation written. For the next two years I was a curate in a depressed area of Liverpool, and the thesis had to be written in the periods left free by parish work. This was not always easy, though to be honest I had to admit that as a part-time philosopher in Liverpool I was not very much more distracted from thesis-writing than during life in Oxford as a full-time student. Eventually I completed the dissertation in 1961, and was orally examined in Oxford by David Pears and Patrick Gardiner. They thought well of the thesis, and I was awarded the doctorate. Apart from the change to a more sexy title, it did not need much alteration to be made ready for publication. I was delighted that Routledge and Kegan Paul agreed to publish it in the series *Studies in Philosophical Psychology* which had been inaugurated by a work I much admired, *Mental Acts* (1957), written by Anscombe's husband Peter Geach. It was published under the title *Action, Emotion and Will*.

After two further years in the priesthood I decided, belatedly, that I could no longer continue as a teacher of doctrines and moral precepts about whose validity I was increasingly doubtful. John Carmel Heenan had now succeeded Cardinal Godfrey as Archbishop of Liverpool, and with his support I obtained leave from Pope Paul VI to return to the lay state. On the strength of *Action, Emotion and Will* I was able without much delay to obtain academic posts in Oxford, first as a lecturer at Exeter and Trinity Colleges and then at Balliol College, where I became a Fellow and tutor in philosophy in 1963.

Action, Emotion and Will, though overwhelmingly influenced by Wittgenstein, also drew on Aquinas's philosophical psychology at a number of points. Shortly after writing it, I translated sections of the *Summa Theologiae* for the new Blackfriars edition that was being brought out by my English Dominican friends. One of the first books I published after obtaining a full-time philosophy post was *The Five Ways* (1969), a study of the celebrated proofs for the existence of God offered by St Thomas at the beginning of the *Summa*. My inquiry led to a negative conclusion: none of the five proofs was a success, because their premises often depended on the assumptions of medieval science, and their arguments sometimes contained identifiable fallacies.

In 1965 I married Nancy Caroline Gayley from Swarthmore, Pennsylvania, whom I had first met in the previous year when she was in Oxford as a member of a choir touring from Vassar College. My marriage, along with the two sons born to us, has ever since been the greatest source of my happiness. As a result of my marrying without a papal dispensation I was automatically excommunicated by the Catholic Church. I have respected the excommunication, in the sense that I have never since taken communion or approached a sacrament. But I am happy to say that my excommunication made no dent in my friendships with my former clerical colleagues. In October 2005 I helped them to celebrate in Rome the golden jubilee of their ordination.

From 1969 to 1972 I was the Wilde Lecturer in Natural Religion in Oxford. A Wilde Lecturer has to give three courses over three years, and I chose to lecture on the divine attributes: one year on omniscience, one on omnipotence and one on benevolence. I argued that these three attributes were incompatible with one another, as could be seen by reflection on the relationship between divine power and human freedom. If God is to be omniscient about future human actions, then determinism must be true. If God is to escape responsibility for human wickedness, then determinism must be false. So there cannot be an omniscient, omnipotent, all good being. I concluded that there can be no such thing as the God of scholastic or rationalist philosophy. I left the question open whether it is possible to conceive, and believe in, a God defined in less absolute terms.

I pursued this question further while Stanton Lecturer at Cambridge between 1980 and 1983. In one series of lectures I presented what I regarded, and regard, as the strongest argument for the existence of some kind of deity, the argument from design. In another series I presented what I regarded, and regard, as the strongest argument against the existence of any God, namely the difficulty of conceiving of a truly disembodied mind. I also gave lectures on the relationship between faith and reason, arguing that religious faith, in the sense of a belief in certain propositions on the alleged word of God, is not a virtue but a vice unless the existence of God can be rationally justified without appeal to faith, and unless the historical events claimed to constitute a revelation can be shown to be historically certain. The themes of these Stanton lectures – which were later repeated in an abbreviated form as Bampton Lectures at Columbia University in New York – are taken up in later chapters of this book.

Reflection in later years has made me more rather than less doubtful about the possibility of the existence of anything to which one can seriously attribute the predicates out of which the traditional notion of Godhead is constructed. At the same time, I have become more interested in assessing the significance of religious discourse interpreted in metaphorical and poetic mode rather than in a literal and scientific manner. I recently collected a number of essays developing these themes in *The Unknown God* (2004).

After 14 years as a philosophy tutor at Balliol I became Master of the College in 1978, and from that date until my retirement I was an academic administrator rather than a teacher. After 11 years as Master of Balliol I retired and became Warden of Rhodes House, responsible for the world-wide programme of Rhodes Scholarships. While holding each of these posts I was a member of the governing Council of the University of Oxford, and after retiring from Rhodes House I was briefly Oxford's Pro-Vice-Chancellor for Development. Since 2001 I have been fully retired and have once again ample time for writing and for reflection.

I recorded the evolution of my religious opinions in a volume of autobiography: *A Path from Rome* (1985). Since 1980 there has in fact been little change in my position on the most fundamental religious issues, but I have written a number of books that touch more or less directly on religious topics. In 1980, for instance, I wrote a brief book on St Thomas Aquinas in Oxford's *Past Master* series. In that book, after a chapter summarizing the Saint's life and works, I wrote a chapter on Being and a chapter on Mind. Aquinas's philosophy of mind, I maintained, deserved as serious consideration as any theory of mind currently on the philosophical market. But the Saint's thesis that God was self-subsistent Being, I argued, could not be rescued from the charge of sophistry and illusion. I expanded the claims made in these two brief chapters in two full-length books, *Aquinas on Mind* (1993) and *Aquinas on Being* (2002).

For reasons unconnected with religion I became interested, during the 1980s, in the statistical study of literary style with the aid of the computer. When I was chosen as the Speaker's Lecturer in Biblical Studies at Oxford from 1980 to 1983 I applied stylometric techniques to the books of the New Testament. From my statistical analysis I drew two conclusions. First, against the consensus of liberal critics, there was no stylistic reason to doubt that the great majority of the Pauline Epistles were written by a single, versatile author. Second, against the fundamentalist orthodoxy, it was highly unlikely that the Apocalypse was written by the same person as the fourth Gospel: no two books of the New Testament were so distant from each other in style as those two.

Having written a *Past Master* on Aquinas, I also contributed two more to the series: *Thomas More* (1983) and *Wyclif* (1985). The Catholic martyr and the condemned heretic were both, in my view, admirable and opposite representatives of the variety of Christian commitment in the years preceding the disastrous and unnecessary division of Christendom at the Reformation.

While at Balliol I became interested in the life and writing of a Balliol poet of the nineteenth century, Arthur Hugh Clough. I was struck by a number of points in which my life had resembled his. Besides the Balliol connection, we were both born in Liverpool and both married our wives after a year of courtship by transatlantic letter. More importantly, we had both detached ourselves, slowly and painfully, from the Christian and clerical constraints of our upbringing. Clough's religious verse, I argued in the book *God and Two Poets* which compared him with Gerard Manley Hopkins, was the finest poetic expression of reverent agnosticism. I became more and more engaged with Clough's poetry, at a time when I became ever-more convinced that all religious language is best interpreted in poetic mode. My most recent book is a full-length biography: *Arthur Hugh Clough, A Poet's Life* (2005).

2

Why I am a Philosopher

For most of my life I have been engaged in the study of philosophy, and I discovered early on that it is simultaneously the most exciting and frustrating of subjects. It is exciting because it is the broadest of all disciplines, since it explores the basic concepts which run through all our talking and thinking. It is frustrating because its great generality makes it extremely difficult: not even the greatest philosophers have succeeded in reaching a complete and coherent understanding even of the language that we use to think our simplest thoughts. The man who is, as it were, the patron saint of philosophers, Socrates, claimed that the only way in which he surpassed others in wisdom was that he was aware of his own ignorance.

It is not possible to explain in advance what philosophy is about: the best way to learn it is to read the works of the great philosophers of the past. Philosophy does not require any special preliminary training and can be undertaken by anyone who is willing to think hard and follow a line of reasoning. To be sure, a course of mathematical logic may discipline a novice philosopher in the same way as a regime of five-finger exercises may help to train a budding pianist. But many of the profoundest questions of philosophy are still beyond the reach of formal logic.

Philosophy is not a matter of expanding knowledge, of acquiring new truths about the world; the philosopher is not in possession of information that is denied to others. Philosophy is not a matter of knowledge, it is a matter of understanding, that is to say, of organizing what is known. But because philosophy is so all-embracing, so universal in its field, the organization of knowledge it demands is something so difficult that only genius can do it. For all of us who are not geniuses, the only way in which we can hope to come to grips with philosophy is by reaching up to the mind of some great philosopher of the past.

In my first years as a professional philosopher, I attempted to make original discoveries in some areas of philosophy, such as the theory of action and the problem of free-will and determinism. After I had written a few books in this area, however, I realized that I was not able enough to compete with the best of my philosophical colleagues. I came to see that the best contribution I could make to the subject was to provide introductions, in contemporary terms, to the great philosophers of the past. For the last 30 years, therefore,

I have written principally about the history of philosophy. The canonical philosophers I most admire, and from whom I have learnt most, are Plato, Aristotle, Augustine, Aquinas, Descartes and Kant. Of the philosophers of our own time, Wittgenstein is for me by far the most insightful.

It is from Wittgenstein that I derived my own under-standing of the nature of philosophy. 'Philosophy is not one of the natural sciences' he wrote in his *Tractatus Logico-Philosophicus* (4.III). 'The word "philosophy" must mean something which stands above or below, but not beside the natural sciences.' He insisted that philosophical problems were to be solved not by the amassing of new empirical knowledge, but by the rearrangement of what we already know. Philosophy seeks not information nor explanation, but understanding.

For centuries it was traditional to see philosophy as the handmaid of theology. More recently it has been fashionable to quote Locke's dictum that philosophy is an underlabourer removing the rubbish that gets in the way of science. But philosophy itself is neither science nor theology, though historically it has been entwined with both. In many areas philosophical thought grew out of religious reflection and grew into empirical science. Many issues which in the past were discussed by philosophers would nowadays be regarded as the province of science: the structure of matter and the history of the cosmos, for instance. If the philosophers of today have a special claim to be the heirs of the great Greek philosophers, it is because unlike the physicists, the astronomers, the medics, the linguists and the theologians, today's philosophers pursue the same goals as Plato and Aristotle only by the same methods as were already available to them.

To illustrate the relationships between religion, philosophy and science, we may consider an area of study given an honoured place by Aristotle under the title of 'theology'. When today we read what he says, the discipline appears a mixture of astronomy and philosophy of religion. Christian and Muslim Aristotelians added to it elements drawn from the teaching of their sacred books. It was when St Thomas Aquinas, in the thirteenth century, drew a sharp distinction between natural and revealed theology that the first important fission took place, removing from the philosophical agenda any appeal to revelation. It took rather longer for the astronomy and the natural theology to separate out from each other.

This example shows that philosophy may give rise to other disciplines by fission. In a similar manner, the seventeenth-century philosophical debate about innate ideas split into a psychological problem (how much is heredity and how much is environment?) and a more precise philosophical problem (how much is *a priori* and how much *a posteriori*?). This second philosophical problem in its turn gave rise to a problem decidable by mathematical logic, and a philosophical residue awaiting further refinement. A discipline remains philosophical as long as its concepts are unclarified, and its methods are controversial. Once agreement is reached about methods, and concepts are given precise definitions, then we have a science setting up house independently of philosophy.

This view of the nature of philosophy, which I have developed from the insights of Wittgenstein, is not at all uncontroversial. After Wittgenstein's death, W. V. Quine of Harvard was widely regarded as the doyen of Anglophone philosophy. Quine attacked the traditional distinction between analytic and synthetic propositions, and this led many philosophers, particularly in the United States, to question whether there was a sharp boundary between philosophy and empirical science.

In particular, there was a drive to amalgamate the philosophy of mind with empirical psychology. This was spearheaded from the philosophical side by Donald Davidson in the quest of a systematic theory of meaning for natural languages, and from the side of linguistics by Noam Chomsky with successive theories postulating hidden mechanisms underlying everyday grammar. The culmination of these developments in the philosophy of mind has been the proclamation of a new cognitive science which will combine the results of philosophy (understood as the study of consciousness) psychology (conceived of on the behaviourist pattern) and neurophysiology (inspired by computational models).

Such scientism – i.e. the attempt to see philosophy as a science – leads philosophers into dead ends. Philosophy is not a part of science, but something that must precede scientific investigation. Suppose a cognitive scientist tells us that he is going to investigate what happens in the brain when we think. We ask him, before starting his research, to be quite sure that he knows what thinking is, what 'think' means. Perhaps he will reply that in order to get clear about the meaning of the word all we have to do is to watch ourselves while we think: what we observe will be what the word means. But if we give serious attention to the ways in which we use the word 'think' we see that this is a misunderstanding of the concept of *thought*. If a neurophysiologist does not have a sound grasp of the concept prior to his investigations, then whatever he discovers, it will not tell us much about thought. He may protest that he is not interested in the linguistic trivialities which entertain philosophers. But after all, he is taking our ordinary language to identify the problem he wants to solve, and to define the boundaries of his research programme. He needs, therefore, to take ordinary language seriously: he should not dismiss it as 'folk-psychology'.

If scientism has blighted philosophy in the United States, on the continent of Europe philosophy has been blown upon by winds from an opposite point of the compass. Philosophy has been assimilated not to science, but to rhetoric. In the work of authors such as Foucault, Derrida and Lacan it is not the line between information and understanding that is deliberately blurred, but the line between rational and irrational modes of persuasion. Argumentation is replaced by devices such as puns, jokes, sneers and incantations. Methods regarded as 'rational' whether in science or philosophy have no objective validity, but merely, according to these writers, reflect the prejudices of some particular hegemonic group.

In fact, it is possible for philosophy to be objectively rational without being a branch of science. Philosophy is, indeed, the quest for rationality across all disciplines, whether sciences, humanities or arts; and its primary method is the attentive study of the language in which these different forms of rationality find their expression. A philosopher studies language, but not as a philologist does. On the one hand, the philosopher has a greater concern with the social practices and institutions in which the language is embedded; on the other hand he/she is not concerned with the idioms and idiosyncracies of particular natural languages, but seeks to identify among their great variety the conceptual structures that underlie them all.

The ambition of philosophy is to reach an understanding of language and the world that transcends particular times and places; but any individual philosopher must accept that he/she will never reach that goal. This has been well put by Thomas Nagel in his book *The View From Nowhere* (1987, OUP). 'Even those who regard philosophy as real and important know that they are at a particular, and we may hope, early stage of its development, limited by their own primitive intellectual capacities, and relying on the partial insights of a few great figures of the past. As we judge their results to be mistaken in fundamental ways, so we must assume that even the best efforts of our own time will come to seem blind eventually' (p. 66).

In his book Nagel urges those of us who are philosophers to combine unashamed pride in the loftiness of our goal with undeluded modesty about the poverty of our achievement, and to resist the temptation to turn philosophy into something less difficult and more shallow than it is. He ends his treatment of philosophical problems with words that have long echoed in my mind. 'I do not feel equal to the problems treated in this book. They seem to me to require an order of intelligence wholly different from mine. Others who have tried to address the central questions of philosophy will recognize the feeling' (ibid.).

3

Why I am Not an Atheist

Many different definitions may be offered of the word
'God'. Given this fact, atheism makes a much stronger
claim than theism does. The atheist says that no matter
what definition you choose, 'God exists' is always false.
The theist claims only that there is some definition
which will make 'God exists' true. In my view, neither
the stronger nor the weaker claim has been convinc-
ingly established.

From time to time philosophers offer proofs, and
disproofs, of the existence of God. More often,
however, theist and atheist philosophers adopt a
strategy that might be called 'grabbing the default
position' – that is to say, a tactic of throwing the burden
of proof on the opponent. But the true default position
is neither theism nor atheism, but agnosticism – that is
to say, the position of one who does not know whether
or not there is a God. A claim to knowledge needs to
be substantiated; ignorance need only be confessed.

WHAT I BELIEVE

From an agnostic position I shall argue in the present chapter that the atheist fails to make good his claim to know that there is no God, and I shall argue in the fourth and fifth chapters that the theist equally fails to present a convincing or coherent demonstration of God's existence. In the remaining chapters I will discuss philosophical and ethical issues without, I hope, begging the question either way.

In order to avoid entering into a discussion of what kind of God they are denying, many atheists prefer to call themselves 'naturalists'. Naturalism is the belief that there is nothing beyond nature, and that everything that exists is part of nature. Naturalism often goes with a commitment to employing in inquiry only the methods of the empirical sciences and mathematics. It entails a denial that there are any spiritual or supernatural entities which are exempt from the laws governing the natural world. It is not, however, as easy as it may appear to give a clear and consistent account of what is meant by 'nature' and 'natural'. Of course, the natural is contrasted with the supernatural; but that contrast by itself will not give us a non-circular account of nature.

At one time the clearest way to delineate naturalism was to identify it with materialism. This was the preferred stance of eighteenth- and early-nineteenth-century atheists. However, developments in microphysics have taken science far away from a world of solid, inert, massy, material atoms. Some atheists, therefore, identify their

22

naturalism not with materialism, but with physicalism; that is the doctrine that everything that happens is determined by the laws of physics. Others, however, realize that such determinism is an implausible thesis when we are trying to give an account of, say, the social behaviour of human beings. On the face of it, while physical processes place causal constraints on human activities, human activities equally exercise top-down causation on physical processes.

The most cautious atheists, therefore, restrict themselves to a purely methodological naturalism, a commitment to employing in inquiry only the methods of the empirical sciences. Because science is an ongoing endeavour, and new methods of research are constantly being devised, naturalism of this kind is perforce an open-ended commitment. But naturalists will claim that the limitations it imposes are not vacuous, since new methods in science always have a continuity with, and a dependence on, the corpus of science each age inherits.

The most fashionable atheists, however, go far beyond this tentative form of naturalism. They claim that the origin and structure of the world and the emergence of human life and human institutions are already fully explained by science, so that no room is left for postulating the existence of activity of any non-natural agent. Their preferred paradigm of explanation is Darwin's account of the origin of species by natural selection.

I have no competence, or wish, to contest the claim that new species have evolved over the ages by processes of natural selection. But when neo-Darwinians offer to explain the entire cosmos, I find problems at three main points: the origin of language, the origin of life and the origin of the universe. I shall try, in the remainder of this chapter, to explain each of my difficulties.

The difficult point about the origin of language arises from the fact that language is conventional. This does not mean that it is set up by a primeval linguistic contract: obviously, one cannot make a contract that a certain word is to mean X unless one already has linguistic means of referring to X. What is meant is rather that the behaviour of language users is rule governed. This is not the same as saying that it is governed by causal laws. Rules differ from laws in several ways. Rules may be broken; short of a miracle causal laws cannot be violated. In order to be governed by a rule, you must be conscious of it at least to the extent that you are aware when it is breached. But to be governed by a causal law there is no need to be conscious of it: there is no reason to believe that the planets are conscious of Kepler's laws.

The problem with the evolutionary account of language is this. Explanation by natural selection of the origin of a feature in a population presupposes the occurrence of that feature in particular individuals of the population. Natural selection might favour a certain length of leg, and the long-legged individuals in the population might outbreed the others. But for this kind of explanation of features to be possible, it must be possible to conceive the occurrence of the feature in single individuals. There is no problem in describing a single individual as having legs n metres long. But there is a problem with the idea that there might be a single-human language-user.

It is not easy to see how the human race may have begun to use language because the language-using individuals among the population were advantaged and so outbred the non-language-using individuals. This is not simply because of the difficulty of seeing how spontaneous mutation could produce a language-using individual; it is the difficulty of seeing how anyone could be described as a language-using individual at all before there was a community of language users. I am using language now in writing, and that I am doing so is no doubt conditioned in all kinds of ways by my own physiology; but the words could not have the meaning they have were it not for the existence of conventions not of my making, and the activities of countless other users of the English language. If we reflect on the social and conventional nature of language, we find something odd in the idea that language may have evolved because of the advantages possessed by language users over non-language users. It seems as absurd as the idea that banks may have evolved because those born with an innate cheque-writing ability were better off than those born without it.

Possibly some non-human animals are capable of being taught language – there is controversy about the success or failure of attempts to do so in recent decades. But even success in teaching language to a chimpanzee would not explain how language came into existence when there was on one to teach it. Language cannot be the result of trial and error learning because such learning presupposes stable goals which successive attempts realize or fail to realize (as a rat may find or fail to find a food pellet in a maze). But there is no goal to which language is a means: one cannot have the goal of acquiring a language, because one needs a language to have that wish in.

If it is difficult to see how language could originate by natural selection, it is equally difficult to see how life could originate that way. However successful natural selection may be in explaining the origin of particular species of life, it clearly cannot explain how there came to be such things as species at all. That is to say, it cannot explain how there came to be true breeding populations, since the existence of such populations is one of the premises on which explanations in terms of natural selection rest as their starting point.

This is not to say that neo-Darwinians do not offer explanations of the origin of life; of course they do, but they are explanations of a radically different kind. All such explanations try to explain life as produced by the chance interaction of non-living materials and forces subject to purely physical laws. These accounts, whatever their merits, are not explanations by natural selection.

Darwin's theory obviously clashes with a literal acceptance of the Bible account of the creation of the world in seven days. Moreover, the length of time which would be necessary for evolution to take place would be immensely longer than the 6,000 years which Christian fundamentalists believe to be the age of the universe. But a non-literal interpretation of Genesis was adopted long ago by theologians as orthodox as St Augustine, and few non-fundamentalist Christians today have any difficulty with the idea that the earth may have existed for billions of years. It is more difficult to reconcile an acceptance of Darwinism with belief in original sin. If the struggle for existence had been going on for aeons before humans evolved, it is impossible to accept that it was man's first disobedience and the fruit of the forbidden tree which brought death into the world.

On the other hand, it is wrong to suggest, as is often done, that Darwin disproved the existence of God. For all Darwin showed, the whole machinery of natural selection may have been part of a Creator's design for the universe. After all, belief that we humans are God's creatures has never been regarded as incompatible with our being the children of our parents; it is no more incompatible with us being, on both sides, descended from the ancestors of the apes.

Natural selection and intelligent design are not incompatible with each other, in the way that natural selection is incompatible with the Genesis story. But though 'intelligent design' may be used in political circles as a euphemism for biblical fundamentalism, in the sheer idea of an extra-cosmic intelligence there is nothing that commits one to a belief in the Judeo-Christian, or any other, religious revelation. To be sure, discussion of the possibility of such an intelligence does not belong in the science classroom; if it did, the intelligence would not be an extra-cosmic one, but a part of nature. But that is no reason why philosophers should not give it serious consideration.

The most fundamental reason in favour of postulating an extra-cosmic agency of any kind is surely the need to explain the origin of the universe itself. It is wrong to say that God provides the answer to the question 'Why is there something rather than nothing?' The question itself is ill conceived: the proposition 'there is nothing' cannot be given a coherent sense, and therefore there is no need to ask why it is false. It is not the existence of the universe that calls for explanation, but its *coming into* existence. At a time when philosophers and scientists were happy to accept that the universe had existed for ever, there was no question of looking for a cause of its origin, only of looking for an explanation of its nature. But when it is proposed that the universe began at a point of time measurably distant in the past, then it seems perverse simply to shrug one's shoulders and decline to seek any explanation. We would never, in the case of an ordinary existent, tolerate a blithe announcement that there was simply no reason for it coming into existence; and it seems irrational to abandon this principle when the existing thing in question is all pervasive, like the universe.

4

Why I am Not a Theist – I

In the 1950s, candidates for a doctorate in Papal universities had to swear to a document called the anti-modernist oath, which contained the statement that it was possible to prove the existence of God. Though I had submitted a dissertation and passed the examinations, I was unwilling to proceed to the degree because I did not wish to take this oath. If God's existence could be known, I very much doubted whether it would be known by way of proof. Since then I have studied arguments for the existence of God presented by many philosophers, and I have not yet found a convincing one.

One of the first thinkers to offer a proof of the existence of the Christian God was St Augustine, and he based his argument on the existence of necessary truths. Such truth, he wrote,

is not the property of any human individual: it is shareable by everyone. Now is this truth superior

31

to, or equal to, or inferior to our minds? If it were inferior to our minds, we would pass judgements about it, as we may judge that a wall is not as white as it should be, or that a box is not as square as it should be. If it were equal to our minds, we would likewise pass judgement on it: we say, for instance, that we understand less than we ought. But we do not pass judgement on the rules of virtue or the truths of arithmetic: we say that the eternal *is* superior to the temporal, and that seven and three *are* ten. We do not say these things *ought* to be so. So the immutable truth is not inferior to our minds or equal to them: it is superior to them and sets the standard by which we judge them. (*De Libero Arbitrio* 2, 12, 34)

So we have found something superior to the human mind and reason. Is this God? Only if there is nothing that is superior to it. If there is anything more excellent than truth, then that is God; if not, then truth itself is God. Whether there is or is not such a higher thing, we must agree that God exists.

In our own time a number of philosophers have offered a similar argument based on the nature of mathematical truth. A realist account of mathematics seems to fail because it is difficult to give a coherent account of numbers as extra-mental entities existing in their own right. On the other hand, any account of mathematics that derives its truths from human mental activities and conventions fails to explain their universality and necessity. The problem may be solved, it is argued, if we treat mathematical entities as existing in the mind of God: they will then be independent of human minds, but not self-standing, extra-mental entities. I do not myself find this argument convincing, but I am not sufficiently competent in the philosophy of mathematics to subject it to adequate philosophical criticism.

The argument from the nature of truth is an interesting one because it falls outside the classification of proofs of God's existence that was made canonical by Kant. According to Kant all arguments to establish the existence of God must take one of three forms. There are ontological arguments, which take their start from the *a priori* concept of a supreme being; there are cosmological arguments, which derive from the nature of the empirical world in general; and there are physico-theological proofs, which start from particular natural phenomena. Proofs in all three classes, according to Kant, were doomed to failure. In every kind of proof, he said, reason 'stretches its wings in vain, to soar beyond the world of sense by the mere might of speculative thought'.

The ontological argument, as Kant sets it out, begins with a definition of God as an absolutely necessary being. Such a being is a thing whose non-existence is impossible. But can we really make sense, he asks, of such a definition? Necessity really belongs to propositions, not to things; and we cannot transfer the logical necessity of a proposition such as 'a triangle has three angles' and make it a property of a real being. Logical necessity is only conditional necessity: nothing is absolutely necessary.

If the ontological argument is valid, then 'God exists' is an analytic proposition: 'exist' is a predicate that is tacitly contained in the subject 'God'. But Kant insists that all statements of real existence are synthetic: we cannot derive actual reality from pure concepts. We might object that we can at least argue from concepts to non-existence: it is because we grasp the concepts *square* and *circle* that we know there are no square circles. If 'square circles do not exist' is analytic, why not 'there is a necessary being'?

A more serious objection to the ontological argument is not that 'God exists' is a synthetic proposition, but that it is not a subject-predicate proposition at all. 'God is omnipotent' contains two concepts linked by the copula 'is'. But in saying 'God exists' or 'there is a God' I add no new predicate to the concept of God, I merely affirm the existence of the subject with all its predicates. As Kant puts it, I posit the object corresponding to my concept.

Existential propositions do not, in fact, always 'posit', because they may occur as sub-clauses in a larger sentence (as in 'If there is a God, sinners will be punished'). But it is true that neither the affirmation nor the supposition of God's existence adds anything to the predicates that make up the concept of God. This point is correct whether or not any particular concept of God is coherent or not (as Kant thought *necessary being* was not). Even if we allow that God is possible, there remains the point that Kant memorably expressed by saying that 100 real dollars contain no more than 100 possible dollars.

Abelard in the twelfth century, and Frege in the nineteenth century, urged us to rephrase statements of existence so that 'exists' does not even look like a predicate. 'Angels exist' should be formulated as 'Some things are angels'. This has the advantage that it does not make it appear that when we say 'Angels do not exist' we are first positing angels and then rejecting them. But it does not settle the issues surrounding the ontological argument, because the problems about arguing from possibility to actuality return as questions about what counts as 'something'. We must ask whether we are including in our consideration possible as well as actual objects.

Thus, some recent philosophers have tried to restate the ontological argument in a novel way, by including possible objects within the range of discussion. A necessary being, they argue, is one that exists in all possible worlds. So defined, a necessary being must exist in our world, the actual world. Our world would not exist unless it were possible; so if God exists in every possible world he must exist in ours.

In this form, the ontological argument – until yesterday the deadest of all duds in the arsenal of the natural theologian – has regained a certain degree of popularity. I myself believe that the notion of possible worlds which provides its framework is philosophically incoherent. But it has to be admitted that such possible world semantics are nowadays the stock-in-trade of the average atheist student of modal logic.

Despite the resurrection of the ontological argument, I believe that Kant was right to insist that whether there is something in reality corresponding to my concept of a thing cannot itself be part of my concept. A concept has to be determined prior to being compared to reality, otherwise we would not know *which* concept was being compared and found to correspond, or maybe not correspond, to reality. *That* there is a God cannot be part of what we mean by 'God'; hence, 'there is a God' cannot be an analytic proposition, and the ontological argument must fail.

However, Kant overestimated the force of his criticism. He maintained that the refutation of the ontological argument carried with it the defeat of the much more popular proof of God's existence from the contingency of the world. That argument, a cosmological argument, is thus briskly set out by Kant in his *Critique of Pure Reason*.

If anything exists, an absolutely necessary being must also exist. Now I, at least, exist. Therefore an absolutely necessary being exists. The minor premise contains an experience, the major premise the inference from their being any experience at all to the existence of the necessary. The proof therefore really begins with experience and is not wholly *a priori* ontological. For this reason, and because the object of all possible experience is called the world, it is entitled the *cosmological* proof. (A 605)

Kant argues that the appeal to experience here is illusory; the force of the cosmological derives only from the ontological argument. For what is meant by 'necessary being'? Surely, a being in whom essence involves existence, that is to say, a being whose existence can be established by the ontological argument. But here Kant ignores the possibility of a different definition of 'necessary being' as meaning a being which can neither come into nor go out of existence, nor suffer change of any kind. Such in fact was the standard account of necessary being given by medieval philosophers who, like Kant, rejected the ontological argument. Such a being may well be regarded as sufficiently different from the caused, variable and contingent items in the world of experience to provide the necessary stable grounding for our fragile and fleeting cosmos.

Such was the notion of necessary being adopted by St Thomas Aquinas, whose Five Ways, placed near the beginning of the *Summa Theologiae* (Ia, 2, 3), are some of the best-known proofs of God's existence. The first four of them are all versions of the cosmological argument. (1) Motion in the world is only explicable if there is a first, motionless mover. (2) The series of efficient causes in the world must lead to an uncaused cause. (3) Contingent and corruptible beings must depend on an independent and incorruptible being. (4) The varying degrees of reality and goodness in the world must be approximations to a subsistent maximum of reality and goodness.

None of these four of the Five Ways is successful as a proof of God's existence: each one contains either a fallacy, or a premise that is false or disputable. The First Way depends on the premise that whatever is in motion is moved by something else: a principle universally rejected since Newton. The series mentioned in the Second Way is not a series of causes through time (which Aquinas himself admitted could reach backwards for ever), but a series of simultaneous causes, like a man moving a stone by moving a crowbar; we are given no reason why the first cause in such a series should be God rather than an ordinary human being. The Third Way contains a fallacious inference from 'Every thing has some time at which it does not exist' to 'there is some time at which nothing exists'. The

Fourth Way depends on a Platonic, and ultimately incoherent, notion of Being.

Many attempts have been made, and no doubt will
be made, to restate these proofs in a manner which
eliminates false premises and fallacious reasoning.
Aquinas's most promising cosmological argument, in
fact, is presented not in the *Summa Theologiae* but in
the *Summa contra Gentiles*. The argument runs thus.
Every existing thing has a reason for its existence,
either in the necessity of its own nature, or in the
causal efficacy of some other beings.

Suppose that A is an existing, natural thing, a
member of a (perhaps beginningless) series of causes
and effects that in its own nature is disposed indifferently to either existence or non-existence. The reason
for A's existing must be in the causal efficacy of other
beings. However many beings may be contributing to
A's present existence, they could not be the reason for
it if there were not some first cause at the head of the
series – something such that everything other than it
must be traced back to it as the cause of its being.

Persuasive as it is, this argument contains a key
weakness. What is meant by saying that A is 'disposed
indifferently to either existence or non-existence'? If it
means 'disposed indifferently to going on existing or
not', then the contingent beings of the everyday world,
from which the argument starts, do not fit the bill.
Contingent things aren't of their nature equally

disposed to exist or not: on the contrary, most things naturally tend to remain in existence. On the other hand, if it means 'disposed indifferently to come into existence or not', then we lapse into absurdity: before A exists there isn't any such thing as a non-existing A to have, or to lack, a tendency to come into existence.

In the *Summa Theologiae* Aquinas's Fifth Way stands apart from the other four ways, and is much the most persuasive of his arguments. It argues that the ordinary teleology of non-conscious agents in the universe entails the existence of an intelligent universal orderer. This is sometimes called 'the argument from design', and it falls into the class of what Kant called 'physico-theological proofs'. This argument, Kant says, must always be mentioned with respect. He himself states it with great eloquence. Everywhere in the world we find signs of order, in accordance with a determinate purpose, apparently carried out with great wisdom. Since this order is alien to the individual things which constitute the world, we must conclude that it must have been imposed by one or more sublime wise causes, operating not blindly as nature does, but freely as humans do. Kant's argument makes use of the key premise of the Fifth Way: 'things which lack awareness do not tend towards a goal unless directed by something with awareness and intelligence, like an arrow by an archer'. Since Darwin, however, such a claim needs more supporting argument than either Kant or Aquinas is able to offer.

Kant's own criticism of the proof he states concerns not its authority but its scope. The most the argument can prove, he says, is the existence of 'an *architect* of the world who is always very much hampered by the adaptability of the material in which he works, not a *creator* of the world to whose idea everything is subject' (A 627). Many religious believers would be very content to have established beyond reasonable doubt the existence of such a Grand Architect. Others would regard the worship of anything less than a creator as being a form of idolatry.

5

Why I am Not a Theist – II

Kant did not say his last word about God in the *Critique of Pure Reason*. In a later work he sets out a number of postulates of practical reason: assumptions that must be made if obedience to the moral law is to be made a rational activity. The postulates turn out to be the same as the traditional topics of natural metaphysics: God, freedom and immortality. We have an obligation to pursue perfect goodness, which includes both virtue and happiness. We can only have an obligation to pursue something if it is possible of achievement: '*ought*', Kant said memorably, 'implies *can*'. But only an all-powerful, omniscient God could ensure that virtue and happiness can coincide – and even such a God can only do so if there is a life after the present one. Hence, it is morally necessary to assume the existence of God.

Kant insisted that there is no inconsistency between this claim and his denial in the first critique that speculative reason could prove the existence and attributes of God. The postulation of God's existence demanded by the moral life is an act of faith. A critical approach to metaphysics was actually a necessary condition of a morally valuable belief in God's existence. 'I have to deny knowledge', he said, 'in order to make room for faith. The dogmatism of metaphysics – the idea that it is possible to make progress in the subject without criticising pure reason – is the true source of that dogmatic unbelief which is at odds with morality.'

Kant's postulation of God as a condition of moral behaviour is something quite different from the attempts at proof we have hitherto considered. The new strategy urges us to believe that God exists not because we have reason to think that 'God exists' is true, but because it is a proposition that is good for us to believe. Perhaps the first exponent of this tactic was the ancient Stoic philosopher Zeno, who argued thus: One of Zeno's most original, if least convincing, arguments went like this. 'You may reasonably honour the gods. But you may not reasonably honour what does not exist. Therefore gods exist.'

This recalls an argument I once came across in a discussion of the logic of imperatives: 'Go to church. If God does not exist, do not go to church. Therefore, God exists'. We are used to hearing prohibitions on deriving an 'ought' from an 'is'. It is less usual to find philosophers seeking to derive an 'is' from an 'ought'. However, throughout the ages philosophers have been eager to derive an 'is not' from an 'ought not': those who have propounded the problem of evil have been in effect arguing that the world ought not to be as it is, and therefore there is no God.

The most plausible exponent of the Zenonian strategy was Blaise Pascal. Pascal admits that by the natural light of reason we are incapable not only of knowing what God is, but even if there is a God at all. But the believer is not left without resource. He addresses the unbeliever thus.

> Either God exists or not. Which side shall we take? Reason can determine nothing here. An infinite abyss separates us, and across this infinite distance a game is being played, which will turn out heads or tails. Which will you bet? (*Pensées*, Penguin edn 1995, no. 680)

You, the unbeliever, perhaps prefer not to wager at all. But you cannot escape: the game has already begun and all have a stake. The chances, so far as reason can show, are equal on either side. But the outcomes of the possible bets are very different. Suppose you bet your life that God exists. If you win, God exists, and you gain infinite happiness; if you lose, then God does not exist and what you lose is nothing. So the bet on God is a good one. But how much should we bet? If you were offered three lives of happiness in return for betting your present life, it would make sense to take the offer.

But in fact what you are offered is not just three life-times but a whole eternity of happiness, so the bet must be infinitely attractive. We have been assuming that the chances of winning or losing a bet on God are fifty-fifty. But the proportion of infinite happiness, in comparison with what is on offer in the present life, is so great that the bet on God's existence is a solid proposition even if the odds against winning are enormous, so long as they are only finite.

Is it true, as Pascal assumes, that one cannot suspend judgement about the existence of God? In the absence of a convincing proof either of theism or of atheism, is not the rational position that of the agnostic, who refuses to place a bet either way? Pascal claims that this is tantamount to betting against God. That may be so, if in fact there is a God who has commanded us under pain of damnation to believe in him: but that should be the conclusion, not the starting point of the discussion.

What is it, in fact, to bet one's life on the existence of God? For Pascal, it meant leading the life of an austere Jansenist. But if reason alone can tell us nothing about God, how can we be sure that that is the kind of life that he will reward with eternal happiness? Perhaps we are being invited to bet on the existence, not just of God, but of the Jansenist God. But then the game is no longer one in which there are only two possible bets: someone may ask us to bet on the Jesuit God, or the Calvinist God, or the God of Islam. Pascal's ingenious apologetic does not succeed in its task: but it does draw attention to the fact that it is possible to have good reasons for believing in a proposition quite separate from reasons that provide evidence for its truth. This consideration was to be developed in more elaborate ways by later philosophers of religion, such as Søren Kierkegaard and John Henry Newman.

In the last century many theist philosophers, convinced by criticisms such as those of Kant, abandoned the search for proofs of God's existence. They began to worry not so much that theological statements might be false, but that they might be meaningless. The rise of linguistic philosophy – often identified with logical positivism in the minds of theologians – convinced a number of Christian philosophers that the traditional notion of God was meaningless or self-contradictory. Some drew the conclusion 'so much the worse for the notion of God' and attempted to devise a Christian atheism; some drew the conclusion 'so much the worse for the principle of non-contradiction' and glorified absurdity with the claim that God was above logic. Neither spectacle was edifying. Those who resisted these follies went on the defensive. Their aim was not so much to show that religion was true as that it was meaningful at all.

Atheist philosophers of religion on the other side were more self-confident, but no more fertile. A chapter of A. J. Ayer's juvenile *Language, Truth, and*

Logic (Gollancz, 1936) and four pages on theology and falsification by Antony Flew called forth a hundred articles of defensive commentary and tentative refutation. But the positivist criteria by which these writers judged theology meaningless had already been abandoned by everyone except theologians. Many of the best-known analytic philosophers were atheists, but if (as was rare) they justified their atheism in their professional writings they tended to do so with arguments drawn, with little modification, from the works of Hume and Kant.

My own conviction that the traditional notion of God could not be defended started from a different point – from the age-old problem of how God can foresee free human actions. In the ancient world both Augustine and Boethius raised the question: if God has foreseen from all eternity that I am going to sin tomorrow, then it cannot be possible for me not to sin tomorrow; but if it is not possible for me not to sin tomorrow how can I be blamed for sinning? Boethius sought to solve the problem in the following way. God lives not in time but in eternity, which he defined as 'the whole and perfect possession, all at once, of endless life'. If God is outside time it is a mistake to speak of him *foreseeing* human actions. His vision of our sins does not constrain them in the way in which some past cause of them might do so.

Boethius's treatment of freedom, foreknowledge and eternity became the classical account for much of the

Middle Ages. But problems remain with his solution of the dilemma he posed with such unparalleled clarity. Surely, matters really are as God sees them; so if God sees my tomorrow's sin as present, then it really is present already. Again, the notion of eternity raises more problems than it solves. If Boethius's imprisonment is simultaneous with God's eternity, and God's eternity is simultaneous with the sack of Troy, does that not mean that Boethius was imprisoned while Troy was burning? We cannot say that the imprisonment is simultaneous with one part of eternity, and the sack with another part, because eternity has no parts but, according to Boethius, happens all at once.

However, many philosophers are willing to accept that human freedom is compatible with determinism. Most of them have in mind the determination of human actions by physical or psychological causation; but if their argument is correct, then human actions can be free even if predetermined by divine decree rather than by terrestrial causation. Though I am not myself a determinist, I am inclined to believe that the compatibilism defended by these philosophers is probably correct. But if freedom is compatible with determinism, then God, by determining human beings, can know what they would do. Human freedom, then, is compatible with divine omniscience.

Nonetheless, it is not possible to reconcile the freedom of the will with the attributes that Christians

49

traditionally ascribe to God. Consider the following article from a confession of faith.

> We believe that the same good God, after He had created all things, did not forsake them or give them up to fortune or chance, but that He rules and governs them according to His holy will, so that nothing happens in this world without His appointment; nevertheless God is neither the Author of nor can be charged with the sins that are committed.

That is a text from the Calvinist Belgic Confession; but orthodox Catholics would agree with every word of it.

I have argued in several places that there cannot be any such thing as the God so described. If determinism is false, and free actions are contingent, then there can be no infallible knowledge of future free actions, since as long as they are future there is no necessity about their happening, and any prediction of them must have an element of conjecture. On the other hand, if determinism is true, then God is indeed the author of sin, because if an agent freely and knowingly sets in motion a deterministic process with a certain upshot, then the agent is responsible for that upshot.

Determinism may be true without that entailing that everything in the world happens by God's intention; our sins may not be the result of God's intentions but only their inevitable outcome. But agents are responsible for their merely voluntary as well as their intentional actions, and in a totally deterministic world the distinction between causing and permitting would have no application to an omnipotent God. Since determinism is either true or false, there cannot be a God who is not the author of sin but infallibly knows future free actions.

The definition of God implied in the Belgic Confession and other Christian creeds is not the only possible definition of God, and it might be possible to avoid an atheist conclusion by offering some different account of God. John Stuart Mill, who rejected the cosmological and ontological arguments for God's existence, was sufficiently impressed by the argument from design to believe that there might well be an entity, less than omnipotent, which deserved the name of 'God'.

'In the present state of our knowledge', he wrote, 'the adaptations in Nature afford a large balance of probability in favour of creation by intelligence'. He did not, however, regard the evidence as rendering even probable the existence of an omnipotent and benevolent creator. An omnipotent being would have no need of the adaptation of means to ends that provides the support of the design argument; and an omnipotent being that permitted the amount of evil we find in the world could not be benevolent. His essay *Theism* (1887) concludes as follows.

These, then, are the net results of natural theology on the question of the divine attributes. A being of great but limited power, how or by what limited we cannot even conjecture; of great and perhaps unlimited intelligence, but perhaps also more narrowly limited power than this, who desires, and pays some regard to, the happiness of his creatures, but who seems to have other motives of action which he cares more for, and who can hardly be supposed to have created the universes for that purpose alone. Such is the deity whom natural religion points to, and any idea of God more cap-tivating than this comes only from human wishes, or from the teaching of either real or imaginary revelation. (Mill, 1887, p. 94)

In my view, there are overwhelming difficulties even with Mill's modest conception of God. If we are to attribute intelligence to any entity – limited or unlim-ited, cosmic or extra-cosmic – we have to take as our starting point our concept of intelligence as exhibited by human beings: we have no other concept of it. Human intelligence is displayed in the behaviour of human bodies and in the thoughts of human minds. If we reflect on the actual way in which we attribute mental predicates such as 'know', 'believe', 'think', 'design', 'control' to human beings, we realize the immense difficulty there is an applying them to a putative being which is immaterial, ubiquitous and eternal. It is not just that we do not, and cannot, know what goes on in God's mind; it is that we cannot really ascribe a mind to God at all. The language that we use to describe the contents of human minds operates within a web of links with bodily behaviour and social institutions. When we try to apply this language to an entity outside the natural world, whose scope of operation is the entire universe, this web comes to pieces, and we no longer know what we are saying.

6

Religion

If science and philosophy cannot settle, one way or the other, the question of the existence of God, must that be the end of the matter? Cannot one appeal above reason to faith, and simply accept the testimony of a sacred text, or of a religious community? Certainly one can: but should one?

Let us consider first the question of the authority of sacred texts. Judaism, Christianity and Islam are all 'religions of the book'. The books of the Torah, the histories of Israel and the writings of the prophets and psalmists provide the bedrock of Jewish religion. The same books are accepted by Christians as the word of God: an Old Testament, to find its culmination in the New Testament unfolded in the Gospels, and the Acts and Epistles of the Apostles. Not only do Jews and Christians share a common heritage, but Christianity and Islam, too, have much in common. Both religions are monotheistic and universalist. Both traditions recognize the Hebrew scriptures as inspired texts, bearing a message from God that has been superseded by a later, definitive, revelation. Members of all three faiths appeal to their own sacred texts to guide or justify their actions of the present day, and within each tradition there are many different methods and procedures by which the ancient sayings are linked to the conditions of modern life. Within these common beliefs and structures there are also highly significant differences of religious and moral teaching.

The authority of sacred texts, if they are to be taken as guides to practical life, is inseparable from the authority of the religious communities and officials whose role is to interpret them. In the Judaeo-Christian tradition, for instance, the very notion of 'the Bible' as a single entity depends on the various authorities throughout history who have established the canon. Within Judaism, at different times and places, the Hebrew Bible has been considered as containing only the Torah, or as extending to include apocryphal writings. The extent of the Christian canon has been a matter of controversy over the centuries and between denominations. Sunni and Shia who share a common allegiance to the Quran can yet engage in mortal religious conflict with each other.

However impressive individual books of the Bible may be, to see them as being elements of a single revelation that contains also some or all of the other books is already tacitly to accept a religious authority which defines a canon. One might gather together the works of Homer, Hesiod, Aeschylus, Sophocles, Euripides, Herodotus and Thucydides into an epitome of Greek thought. The books would share a common cultural tradition and cohere with each other as well or ill as the books of the Old and New Testament do. But we do not treat them as a single book, to be treated differently from all other books, because there has never been a Hellenic rabbinate or episcopate to adjudicate on their canonicity and impose them as authoritative.

As a community is further in time from the origination of its authoritative texts, the role of the official interpreters of those texts becomes more and more important, and the degree of their control over members of the community increases. This is already clear in the case of comparatively recent texts such as the American Constitution, in which the Supreme Court can detect rights – such as that of privacy – that would have astonished the framers of the Constitution, so far as we can tell from their surviving writings. Much more so is this the case with sacred texts whose origin is ancient and mysterious, and to whose authors' minds we have access only through those texts themselves.

To someone who does not accept the authority of the contemporary interpreters of the canonical scriptures, each individual book must be judged in its own right. Most who look at the texts from a secular viewpoint find them uneven. Some are the work of brilliant writers like Isaiah or St Paul; others, like Leviticus and Revelation are tedious or repellent. Some, like Genesis and Jonah, seem clearly mythical or legendary; others, such as parts of the Books of Kings and the Acts of the Apostles, bear marks of historical authenticity. But without the authority conferred by being part of a defined canon, they clearly cannot be taken together as a coherent whole, since they contain too many contradictions on important issues. The books of the Old Testament do not agree whether the soul survives after death; the books of the New Testament tell different stories about the imminence of the end of the world.

I do not share the extreme scepticism of many scholars, including Christian scholars, about the historical value of the Gospels. For instance, that Jesus at his last meal took bread and wine and said something like 'this is my body, this is my blood' seems to me to be as likely to be true as anything that is narrated in the records of the early Roman Empire. With regard to the Acts of the Apostles, I have long been amused to note that Catholic biblical scholars often appear less ready to accept them as broadly historical than are atheist colleagues in ancient history departments.

Members of religious communities, however, are invited not to survey the sacred books with a critical eye, but to accept their teaching as a matter of faith. It is wrong, however, to make a sharp contrast between faith and reason, and indeed nowadays it is often the proponents of faith who are loudest in their defence of the rights of reason. At least since St Thomas Aquinas the traditional Christian position has been that while some truths are not attainable by reason and can only be accessed by faith in a revelation, no revealed doctrines are contrary to reason and faith itself is a reasonable frame of mind. Every philosopher, it may be argued, atheist as well as theist, brings to his task antecedent convictions, and neither side can claim a monopoly of willingness to follow the argument where it leads. Against this background, it is reasonable to expect, and to accept with faith, a divine revelation.

There is, however, an important difference here between the believer and the unbeliever. An unbeliever can contemplate without guilt the possibility of changing his mind and accepting belief; the believer, on the other hand, holds that it would be sinful for him to change his mind and lose his faith. This does not, in itself, make faith irrational: after all, a secular liberal must surely believe that it would be wicked for him so to change his own mind as to become a Nazi. But it does nullify any claim that the believing philosopher is as open-minded as the unbeliever.

In my view, faith is not a virtue, but a vice, unless certain conditions are fulfilled. One is that the existence of God can be rationally established without appeal to faith. Accepting something as a matter of faith is taking God's word for its truth: but one cannot take God's word for it that He exists. Another is that the historical events that are claimed to constitute the divine revelation must be independently established as historically certain – as having the same certainty, say, as that Charles I was beheaded in London, or that Cicero was once consul in Rome. The events that are pointed to as founding charters for the world's great religions can surely not claim this degree of certainty.

This judgement is, of course, based on a reading of the religious narratives considered just as purported historical records. To argue for the validity of a religious institution on the grounds that its sacred texts have a unique authority would be to argue in a circle, since, as I have pointed out, those texts only have canonical status because it was conferred on them by the institutions in question.

In particular, the authority claimed for the Pope as head of the Church rests on very dubious foundations. The inscription around the dome of the Vatican basilica claims it to be based on the words of Jesus recorded in St Matthew's Gospel 'Thou art Peter and upon this rock I will build my church'. But even if we accept St Matthew's account without question, it is difficult to have confidence in the link between St Peter and the Pope given the lack of any serious evidence that St Peter was ever Bishop of Rome, or indeed a bishop at all.

Of course, any serious person, secular or religious, must respect the Pope as the religious leader of a large proportion of the world's population. But his title to authority within the Church, and respect outside it, must rest not on a partly legendary historical pedigree, but upon the consent of those he governs.

That consent, in recent years, seems to have been considerably weakened. Many, even of Catholics whose religious observance is exemplary, call into question Papal teaching on important moral issues. I must confess that I find it difficult to make logical sense of the position of such Catholic dissidents. At the time of the Second Vatican Council I wrote as follows in a review of a book by liberal Catholics raising objections to Catholic teaching.

Let us suppose the Vatican Council were to declare that despite past teaching, artificial contraception is not intrinsically immoral. How could the Roman Catholic Church ever be taken seriously again as a moral authority? If a doctrine taught so solemnly, and at a cost of such suffering, can turn out to be so mistaken, what reliance can be placed on any other moral doctrine? If the use of contraceptives is ever permissible, it is surely frequently obligatory: in that case many of the faithful must have been kept for years from the performance of their duty by the teaching of the Church.

> If [liberal Catholics] are in the right, then at any time during the last fifty years a man would have been morally and religiously better off outside the Roman Catholic Church than within it. For as a result of being a Catholic he has been seriously misinformed about the nature of marriage, about the authority of the Bible, about the place of the Church and the sacraments, and about the justice and judgements of God. And if this is so, what rational ground has anyone for being a Roman Catholic at all?

That line of argument seems to me as sound as ever. Forty years on, it is easy to add to the list of Catholic teachings which many Catholics find abhorrent: the condemnation of homosexuality, the teaching about the role of women, even the proscription of abortion.

But it is not only traditional moral teaching that is disowned by many Catholics. So too is the doctrine which, if true, is the strongest possible reason for being a Catholic in the first place: namely, the doctrine that membership of the Church is the only way to save one's soul and avoid an eternity of damnation in hell.

For centuries it was the teaching of the Roman Church that the majority of human beings went to hell, and that only Catholics, and most likely only a minority of them, went to heaven. Jesus taught 'Strait is the gate, and narrow is the way, which leadeth unto

life, and few there be that find it'. St Augustine interpreted this, and other texts, as meaning that the human
race was a *massa damnata* out of which only a few elect
were predestined and chosen to be saved and so to
heaven. Pope Boniface VIII concluded his Bull *Unam
Sanctam*, 1302, with the words 'We declare, say, define,
and proclaim to every human creature that if they are
to be saved they must of necessity be subject to the
Roman Pontiff'.

It was not only in the Catholic Church that Christians accepted Augustine's picture of the dreadful future
that awaits the great majority of the human race. After
the disruption of the Reformation, Calvin in the
Protestant camp and Jansenius in the Catholic camp
were to offer visions of even darker gloom; and in the
nineteenth century Kierkegaard and Newman stressed,
like Augustine, how narrow was the gate that gave
entry to the supreme good of final bliss. The breezy
optimism that characterized many Christians in the
twentieth century has little backing from tradition.

The ecumenical rapprochement between the
Churches in recent years, and their recognition of
the validity of other faiths, is obviously something to be
welcomed from a secular point of view since it lessens
the likelihood of religious combat and conflict. But it is
difficult to make coherent with any strong view of the
teaching authority of the Churches. As late as 1950
the Encyclical *Humani Generis* denounced those

theologians who reduced to a vain formula the necessity of belonging to the true Church if one was to attain everlasting salvation. It is difficult for any historical Christian denomination altogether to disown the Athanasian Creed which, having enunciated a very specific doctrine of the Trinity, concludes 'This is the Catholic faith; unless anyone believes this faithfully and firmly, he cannot be saved' and makes plain that those who are not saved pass into eternal fire.

Of course, personally I welcome the amiable inconsistency of my Christian, Catholic and clerical friends. I am delighted that they do not appear to believe that, as an unbeliever, I am destined to an eternity of hell-fire. But I cannot get rid of the feeling that, in the light of the age-long teachings of their Church, they ought to do so.

Membership of a Church is one thing, worship is another. Being agnostic does not mean that one cannot pray. In itself, prayer to a God about whose existence one is doubtful is no more irrational than crying out for help in an emergency without knowing whether there is anyone within earshot. But if, as I have argued, statements about God in the indicative mood cannot be interpreted literally, equally prayers to God cannot be taken as literal uses of the imperative mood either.

Because human beings are social animals, prayer, like other activities, needs a social as well as an individual context. For this reason I am grateful to the Christian communities who, during the course of my life, have allowed me to join in their worship without acknowledging their authority.

7

Human Beings

In the history of philosophy there have been two recurrent contrasting conceptions of what it is to be human. One we may call Aristotelian and the other Cartesian. (Both can trace their ancestry to the polymorphous Plato.) According to Aristotle, a human being is an animal of a particular kind: a rational animal. According to Descartes, a human person is a spirit of a particular kind, temporarily and mysteriously united to a body. I accept the Aristotelian account and regard the Cartesian account as fundamentally mistaken.

In sceptical vein, Descartes believed that he could doubt the existence of the external world and the existence of his own body. He brought his doubt to an end with the famous argument 'cogito, ergo sum – I think, therefore I am'. This led to the question 'What am I?' Descartes's answer was that he was a substance whose whole essence or nature was to think, and whose being required no place and depended on no material thing. He was an immortal mind, linked to a mortal body which was a particularly elaborate machine.

To Descartes's question my own, Aristotelian, answer is that I am a human being, a living body of a certain kind. We sometimes speak as if we have bodies, rather than are bodies. But having a body, in this natural sense, is not incompatible with being a body; it does not mean that there is something other than my body that *has* my body. Just as my body has a head, a trunk, two arms and two legs, but is not something over and above the head, trunk, arms and legs, so I have a body but am not something over and above the body.

As well as a body, I have a mind: that is to say I have various psychological capacities, including especially an intellect and a will. The intellect is the capacity to acquire and exercise intellectual abilities of various kinds, such as the mastery of language and the possession of objective information. The will is the capacity for the free pursuit of goals formulated by the intellect. Intellect and will are not themselves independent entities: they are capacities. What are they capacities of? Of the living human being, the bodily person that you would see if you were here in the room where I write.

You too have a mind and a body, and so do all human beings: that is to say we are all bodies that have certain mental capacities. The intellect and the will are peculiar to human beings, but there are other faculties – the ability to see and hear, for instance, and the capacity for pleasure and pain – that we share with other animals. Descartes believed that only human beings were conscious and that other animals were machines lacking consciousness; but Descartes was wrong.

What is peculiar to our species is the capacity for thought and behaviour of the complicated and symbolic kinds that constitute the linguistic, social, moral, economic, scientific, cultural and other characteristic activities of human beings in society. The mind is a capacity, not an activity: it is the capacity to acquire intellectual abilities of which the most important is the mastery of language. The will, in contrast with animal desire, is the capacity to pursue goals that only language-users can formulate. The study of the acquisition and exercise of language is the way *par excellence* to study the nature of the human mind.

It is because Descartes did not take this fact seriously that his philosophy of mind fell into error. When he tried to doubt everything, the one thing he did not call into question was the meaning of the words he was using in his solitary meditation. Had he done so, he would have had to realize that even the words we use in soliloquy derive their meaning from the social community which is the home of our language, and that therefore it was not, in fact, possible to build up his philosophy from solitary private ideas.

Nowadays it is fashionable to denounce Descartes: almost every writer, whether philosopher or physiologist, begins his discussion of the human mind with a renunciation of Cartesian dualism. But many who are officially anti-Cartesian retain the fundamental erroneous principle that the contents of our minds are accessible to private introspection without reference to the public and social institutions in which our language is embedded.

According to the dualist, the relation between mental processes and their expression in behaviour is a contingent relation; it is not any sort of logical necessity. Mind and body are separate; each of them could in principle live its life independent of the other. At the opposite pole from dualism is behaviourism: the theory that all ascriptions of mental attributes to human beings, if they are not to be mere myth-making, must be reducible to ascriptions of bodily behaviour. Behaviourism is an error no less than dualism. The truth is that bodily behaviour is neither identical with, nor only contingently connected with, the mental life of which it is the expression. Bodily behaviour is not identical with mental life, but only evidence for it; but this evidential relation is one which is built into the meaning of the mental predicates by which we describe the life of human beings.

If that is a fair account of the relationship between the mind and behaviour, what are we to say about the relation between the mind and the brain? To do so we must recall that the mind is a capacity; and we must make a distinction between the possessors of capacities and the vehicles of capacities. The possessor of an ability is what *has* the ability: I am the possessor of my linguistic skills; I am the one (and not my mind or my brain) who knows English and who is exercising that ability in writing this chapter. Similarly, my car has the ability to decelerate; it can reduce speed in answer to my touch on the foot-brake. The *vehicle* of the car's ability to decelerate is the brake mechanism. The vehicle of an ability is that part or feature in virtue of which the possessor of an ability is able to exercise it. A vehicle is something concrete and more or less tangible; an ability, on the other hand, has neither length nor breadth nor location. It is, if you like, an abstraction from behaviour or performance.

We can apply this distinction between possessors, abilities and vehicles to the relation between people, their minds and their brains. Human beings, as we have said, are living bodies of a certain kind who possess various abilities, most notably intellectual abilities. The vehicle of the human mind is, very likely, the human brain (plus other parts of the nervous system).

Human beings and their brains are physical objects; their minds are not, because they are capacities. This does not mean that they are spirits. A round peg's ability to fit into a round hole is not a physical object like the round peg itself, but no one will suggest that it is a spirit. It is not any adherence to dualism, but a simple concern for conceptual clarity, that makes me insist that a mind is not a physical object and does not have a length and a breadth.

So far in this chapter I have spoken of human beings rather than of persons. My reason for doing so is that the concept of 'person' has a strange history. It traces its origin to theological controversies in the early Christian centuries. According to the orthodox doctrine the Father, the Son and the Holy Ghost are each God. But there is only one God. What, then, are there three of? The answer was devised: persons. Again, Jesus was both man and God. Manhood and godhood are different, so Jesus had two distinct natures. But how then were God the Son and Jesus of Nazareth a single thing? Answer: they were the same person. Thus a Latin word once meaning an actor's mask was given a new significance, and a puzzling and profound concept entered metaphysics.

From its origin, then, the concept of person was not quite identical with the concept of human being, since it applied also in the divine realm. But John Locke in the seventeenth century drew a wedge between the two concepts even in the human realm by making a distinction between the identity of persons and the identity of human beings. Tom might be the same person as Dick, he maintained, without being the same man as Dick. For the criteria for A's being the same person as B are mental (roughly, continuity of memory) and the criteria for A's being the same human being as B are physical (roughly, continuity of metabolism). As in the time of Locke, so at the present day the concept of person is a matter of contention in the philosophy of mind.

Which concept we adopt is a matter of practical significance in cases where the treatment of individuals and groups (e.g. fetuses, the insane, the terminally ill) depends on whether they are classified as persons or not. Given that conflicting criteria may be offered in different contexts for deciding whether someone is or is not a person, many philosophers think that the first thing to decide is how the law should treat an individual, and only then go on to decide whether to call such an individual a person.

This seems to me a serious error. It is true that the Lockean concept of person, on investigation, collapses and fragments. But the solution is not to abandon the attempt to give a philosophical, pre-legal account of personhood. It is to accept that Locke took a wrong turn and that his concept was a muddle from the start; that it was a mistake to try to make a distinction, among human beings, between being the same person and being the same man. The concept of a human being – an animal of a particular species with particular capacities – provides us with the only concept of person that we can really understand.

The thesis that we should first decide how the law should treat individuals and only then decide whether they are persons has disastrous effects in policy making. It is used to justify depriving human individuals of human rights. Mercifully we still do talk of 'human rights' – of rights people have just because they are human. We do not talk of 'personal rights' in the sense of rights that people have because some legislator defines them as persons.

The most recent chapter in the history of the English word 'person' has been one of the strangest. While writing these paragraphs I have frequently used the expression 'human being'. Fifty years ago, a writer would unself-consciously have used instead the single word 'man'. It was a defect in the English of the period that, unlike Greek, say, or German, it did not have two different words to indicate a member of the human race and a member of the male gender. Feminists rightly objected to this, and insisted that a distinction be introduced, and that is why 'man' is now much less often used in the sense of 'human'. From the linguistic point of view, I think the wrong option was chosen. It is a pity that women did not insist that 'man' should be used only when it meant 'human' and that if 'man' meant 'male' it should be marked in some way (e.g. 'he-man'). Instead, the females of the species have left the males in possession of the historic name of the race, and introduced new usages to express our common humanity. But the word that has become most popular as the contemporary English equivalent of the Greek *anthropos* and the German *Mensch* is – *pace* John Locke – the word 'person'. So 'person' has after all come home to mean just the same as 'human being'.

8

The Nature of Morality

In later chapters I will discuss particular moral issues of life and death, such as the legitimacy of abortion, euthanasia, warfare and capital punishment. I will also discuss moral questions connected with economics, politics and sex. In the present chapter I want to discuss morality at a more abstract level, asking what is the best ethical system through which to approach concrete moral problems. The discussion may seem arid, but it is of great importance. Philosophical systems exercise an influence which is less obvious, but more enduring, than particular fashions in moral and political correctness.

The most influential ethical system at the present time is utilitarianism, whose foundation is commonly credited to Jeremy Bentham (1748–1832), a gifted jurisprudent whose remains, encased in waxwork, can still be seen in University College London, which he helped to found. The guiding idea of the system is what Bentham called 'the principle of utility' or 'the greatest happiness principle'. The principle of utility evaluates every action according to the tendency which it appears to have to augment or diminish happiness. The promotion of the greatest happiness of the greatest number is the only right and proper end of human action.

Bentham commended the principle of utility by contrasting it with other ethical systems, of which the most striking is the principle of asceticism. The principle of asceticism is the mirror image of the principle of utility, approving of actions to the extent that they tend to diminish the quantity of happiness. Bentham's principle of asceticism sets up a straw man. Religious traditions have indeed set a high value on self-denial and mortification of the flesh; but even among religious teachers it is rare to find one who makes the infliction of suffering upon oneself the overarching principle of every action. No one, religious or secular, has ever proposed a policy of pursuing the greatest misery of the greatest number. Bentham sets himself a more realistic target when he attacks those who say that in order to discover whether something is right we must consult the will of God. We cannot, Bentham says, appeal to the will of God to settle whether something is right; we have to know first whether it is right in order to decide whether it is conformable to God's will.

Bentham himself did not bring out what is the really significant difference between utilitarianism and other moral systems. We may divide moral philosophers into absolutists and consequentialists. Absolutists believe that there are some kinds of action that are intrinsically wrong, and should never be done, irrespective of any consideration of the consequences. Consequentialists believe that the morality of actions should be judged by their consequences, and that there is no category of act which may not, in special circumstances, be justified by its consequences. Prior to Bentham most philosophers were absolutists, because they believed in a natural law, or natural rights. If there are natural rights and a natural law, then some kinds of action, actions that violate those rights or conflict with that law, are wrong, no matter what the consequences.

Bentham rejected the notion of natural law, on the grounds that no two people could agree what it was. He was scornful of natural rights, believing that real rights could only be conferred by positive law; and his greatest scorn was directed to the idea that natural rights could not be over-ridden. 'Natural rights is simple nonsense: natural and imprescriptible rights, rhetorical nonsense – nonsense upon stilts'. If there is no natural law and no natural rights, then no class of actions can be ruled out in advance of the consideration of the consequences of such an action in a particular case.

This difference between utilitarians and previous moralists is highly significant, as can be easily illustrated. For instance, Aristotle, Aquinas and almost all

Christian moralists believed that adultery was always wrong. Not so for Bentham: the consequences foreseen by a particular adulterer must be taken into account before making a moral judgement. Again, a believer in natural law, told that some Herod or Nero has killed 5,000 citizens guilty of no crime, will say without further ado 'that was a wicked act'. A thoroughgoing consequentialist, before making such a judgement, must ask further questions. What were the consequences of the massacre? What did the monarch foresee? What would have happened if he had allowed the 5,000 to live?

Objections to utilitarianism come in two different forms. As a moral code, it may be thought to be too strict, or it may be thought to be too lax. Those who complain that it is too strict say that to insist that in every single action one should take account not just of one's own but of universal happiness is to demand a degree of altruism beyond the range of all but saints. Indeed, even to work out what is the most felicific of the choices available at any given moment calls for superhuman powers of calculation. Those who regard utilitarianism as too lax say that its abolition of absolute prohibitions on kinds of action opens a door for moral agents to persuade themselves whenever they feel like it that they are in the special circumstances which would justify an otherwise outrageous act. Bentham's most distinguished disciple, John Stuart

Mill, wrote to his Platonic lover Harriet Taylor, 'Where there exists a genuine and strong desire to do that which is most for the happiness of all, general rules are merely aids to prudence, in the choice of means; not peremptory obligations. Let but the desires be right, and the "imagination lofty and refined"; and provided there be disdain of all false seeming, "to the pure all things are pure"'.

Defences against such criticisms can be, and have been offered. But there is a more fundamental objection to utilitarianism, pointed out to me by Arthur Prior some 50 years ago. If you are a utilitarian you believe that the correct action to perform is the one which, of all the alternatives open to you will have the best total consequences. Either determinism is true or it is not. If it is, then there is only one course of action which is a genuinely possible choice for us: whatever we do will be the best possible action because the only possible action. If, on the other hand, determinism is false, then there is no such thing as the totality of the consequences of one's action; for the total future of the world depends on the choices of others as well as one's own. Either way, then, utilitarianism offers no decision procedure: it is no help in deciding what we ought to do.

'The greatest happiness of the greatest number' is one of those philosophical slogans, like 'the best of all possible worlds', or 'that than which nothing greater can be conceived' which are impressive on first hearing, but turn out to have no clear meaning. Nonetheless, utilitarianism has made consequentialism widespread among professional philosophers. It is probably more popular in theory than in practice: outside philosophy seminars most people probably believe that some actions are so outrageous that they should morally be ruled out in advance, and reject the idea that one should literally stop at nothing in the pursuit of desirable consequences. But in present-day discussions of, for instance, topics in medical ethics, it is consequentialists who have the greater say in the formation of policy. This is because they talk in the cost-benefit terms that technologists and policy makers instinctively understand.

Moreover, even among the general public many people are suspicious of the idea that some classes of action are absolutely prohibited. Where, they ask, do these absolute prohibitions come from? No doubt religious believers see them as coming from God; but they do not seem to be able to agree among themselves which are the actions that God has prohibited absolutely. Even if they did, how could they convince unbelievers of this? On the other hand, can there be a prohibition without a prohibiter? Do not those who believe that some kinds of action are absolutely ruled out merely express the prejudices of their upbringing?

The answer is to be found in the nature of morality

itself. There are three elements that are essential to morality: a moral community, a set of moral values and a moral code. All three are necessary. First, it is as impossible to have a purely private morality as it is to have a purely private language, and for very similar reasons. Secondly, the moral life of the community consists in the shared pursuit of non-material values, such as fairness, truth, comradeship, freedom. It is the nature of the values pursued that distinguishes morality from economics. Thirdly, this pursuit is carried out within a framework which excludes certain prohibited types of behaviour. It is this that distinguishes morality from aesthetics, which is also a pursuit of non-material values. The answer to the question 'Who does the prohibiting?' is that it is the members of the moral community: membership of a common moral society involves subscription to a common code. The moral community creates moral laws in a manner similar to that in which the linguistic community creates the rules of grammar and syntax. Moral rules, like linguistic rules, may change as society changes; but unless a set of such rules is in operation society collapses into anarchy as language collapses into incoherence.

This conception of the origin of moral rules was picturesquely sketched by Immanuel Kant in his *Groundwork of the Metaphysic of Morals*. Every human being, he said, is a member of a kingdom of ends, a union of rational beings under common laws. My own will is rational only in so far as its maxims – the principles on which it makes its choices – are capable of being made universal laws. The converse of this is that universal law is law that is made by rational wills like mine. A rational being is 'subject only to laws which are made by himself and yet are universal'. In the kingdom of ends, we are all both legislators and subjects.

Kant's moral system is at the opposite pole from Bentham's. The overarching concept in Kantian ethics is not happiness, but duty. The function of reason in ethics is not to inform the will how best to choose means to some further end: it is to produce a will that is good in itself; and a will is good only if it is motivated by duty. Good will, for Kant, is the only thing that is good without qualification. Fortune, power, intelligence, courage and all the traditional virtues can be used to bad ends; even happiness itself can be corrupting. It is not what it achieves that constitutes the goodness of a good will; good will is good in itself alone.

> Even if, by some special disfavour of destiny, or by the niggardly endowment of stepmotherly nature, this will is entirely lacking in power to carry out its intentions, if by its utmost effort it still accomplishes nothing, and only good will is left . . . even then it would still shine like a jewel for its own sake as something which has its full value in itself. (1, 3)

Good will, for Kant, is the highest good and the condition of all other goods, including happiness.

If a will is good only when motivated by duty, we must ask what it is to act out of duty. A first answer is to say that it is to act as the moral law prescribes. But this is not enough. Kant distinguishes between acting in accordance with duty, and acting from the motive of duty. A grocer who chooses honesty as the best policy, or a philanthropist who takes delight in pleasing others, may do actions that are in accord with duty. Such actions conform to the moral law, but they are not motivated by reverence for it. Actions of this kind, however correct and amiable, have, according to Kant, no moral worth. Worth of character is shown only when someone does good not from inclination but from duty. A man who is wholly wretched and longs to die, but preserves his own life solely out of a sense of duty – that is Kant's paradigm of good willing.

Happiness and duty, therefore, are for Kant not just different but conflicting motives. Indeed, it is the painfulness of well-doing that is the real mark of virtue. If virtue brings happiness, that must only be as a by-product. 'The more a cultivated reason concerns itself with the aim of enjoying life and happiness, the farther does man get away from true contentment.' We should not take the Bible seriously when it tells us to love our neighbour: it is cold unfeeling charitable assistance that is really commanded.

While Kant's picture of the kingdom of ends throws light on the nature of morality, his exaltation of duty as the supreme moral motive not only has repelled many modern thinkers, but was also a departure from all previous moral systems. From Plato and Aristotle through the Christian era, moralists had, like Bentham, placed the concept of happiness at the apex of moral reasoning. But unlike Bentham, they believed that it was the moral agent's own happiness, not the happiness of any collectivity, that was the ultimate motive for moral behaviour.

Aristotle was one of the most conspicuous of these philosophers: but because he regarded happiness as consisting in the exercise of human excellences or virtues, most of his famous treatise, the *Nicomachean Ethics* is concerned with virtue – whether it is intellec- tual virtue (by which he means the pursuit of truth and understanding through science and philosophy) or moral virtue (by which he means the characteristics which enable us to pursue a life of good and noble actions).

Moral virtue, for Aristotle, is expressed in good purpose, that is to say, a prescription for action in accordance with a good plan of life. The actions which express moral virtue will, he tells us, avoid excess and defect. A temperate person, for instance, will avoid eating or drinking too much; but he will also avoid eating or drinking too little. Virtue chooses the mean, or middle ground, between excess and defect, eating and drinking the right amount. Aristotle goes through a long list of virtues, beginning with the traditional ones of fortitude and temperance, but including others such as liberality, sincerity, dignity and conviviality, and sketches out how each of them is concerned with a mean.

The doctrine of the mean is not intended as a recipe for mediocrity or an injunction to stay in the middle of the herd. Aristotle warns us that what constitutes the right amount to drink, the right amount to give away, the right amount of talking to do, may differ from person to person, in the way that the amount of food needed by an Olympic champion may not suit a novice athlete. Each of us learns what is the right amount by experience: by observing, and correcting, excess and defect in our conduct.

Virtue, Aristotle tells us, is concerned not only with action but with passion. We may have too many fears or too few fears, and courage will enable us to fear when fear is appropriate and be fearless when it is not. We may be excessively concerned with sex and we may be insufficiently interested in it: the temperate person will take the appropriate degree of interest and be neither lustful nor frigid. Passion was as important as action in the assessment of virtue: people were not really virtuous as long as virtuous action went against the grain. Aristotle's paradigm of a virtuous man was somebody who thoroughly enjoyed carrying out his virtuous endeavours. Such a person is quite different from Kant's cold-blooded duty-doer.

For Aristotle, the virtues, besides being concerned with means of action and passion, are themselves means in the sense that they occupy a middle ground between two contrary vices. Thus courage is in the middle, flanked on one side by foolhardiness and on the other by cowardice; generosity treads the narrow path between miserliness and prodigality. But while there is a mean of action and passion, there is no mean of virtue itself: there cannot be too much of a virtue in the way that there can be too much of a particular kind of action or passion. If we feel inclined to say that someone is too courageous, what we really mean is that his actions cross the boundary between the virtue of courage and the vice of foolhardiness. And if there cannot be too much of a virtue, there cannot be too little of a vice: so that there is no mean of vice any more than there is a mean of virtue.

While all moral virtues are means of action and passion, it is not the case that every kind of action and passion is capable of a virtuous mean. There are some actions of which there is no right amount, because any amount of them is too much: Aristotle gives murder and adultery as examples. There is no such thing as committing adultery with the right person at the right time in the right way. Similarly, there are passions which are excluded from the application of the mean: there is no right amount of envy or spite.

Aristotle's account of virtue as a mean seems to many readers truistic. In fact, it is a distinctive ethical theory which contrasts with other influential systems of various kinds. Moral systems such as traditional Jewish or Christian doctrine give the concept of a moral law (natural or revealed) a central role. This leads to an emphasis on the prohibitive aspect of morality, the listing of actions to be altogether avoided: most of the commands of the Decalogue, for instance, begin with 'thou shalt not'. Aristotle does believe that there are some actions that are altogether ruled out, as we have just seen; but he stresses not the minimum necessary for moral decency but rather the conditions of achieving moral excellence (that is, after all, what *ethike arete* means). He is, we might say, writing a text for an honours degree, rather than a pass degree, in morality.

But it is not only religious systems that contrast with Aristotle's treatment of the mean. For a utilitarian, or any kind of consequentialist, there is no class of actions to be ruled out in advance. On a utilitarian view, since the morality of an action is to be judged by its consequences there can, in a particular case, be the right amount of adultery or murder. On the other hand, some secular ascetic systems have ruled out whole classes of actions: for a vegetarian, for instance, there can be no right amount of the eating of meat. We might say that from Aristotle's point of view utilitarians go to excess in their application of the mean, whereas vegetarians are guilty of defect in its application. Aristotelianism, naturally, hits the happy mean in application of the doctrine.

For many centuries Christian moralists combined the virtue ethics of Aristotle with the initially Hebrew notion of a divine law. The commands and prohibitions of the decalogue set the framework within which the good Christian would pursue happiness in this world and the next through the exercise of the Aristotelian virtues. Some Christian thinkers, however, placed more emphasis on the notion of law, and others placed more emphasis on the notion of virtue.

For St Thomas Aquinas, for instance, while murder, abortion, usury and the like were all violations of the natural law of God, the overall ethical system of the *Summa Theologiae* is structured not around the concept of law, but around the concept of virtue as the route to self-fulfilment in happiness. It was Duns Scotus, at the beginning of the fourteenth century, who gave the theory of divine law the central place that it was to occupy in the thought of Christian moralists henceforth.

Scotus agreed with Aristotle and Aquinas that human beings have a natural tendency to pursue happiness but in addition, he postulated a natural tendency to pursue justice. The natural appetite for justice is a tendency to obey the moral law no matter what the consequences may be for our own welfare. Human freedom for Scotus consisted in the power to weigh in the balance the conflicting demands of morality and happiness.

All Catholic moralists, however, and all Protestant moralists until the Enlightenment agreed that there were some kinds of action that were absolutely ruled out by divine law. They were, in the terms I used earlier, absolutists and not consequentialists. This did not, of course, mean that they paid no account to foreseen and foreseeable consequences in making moral evaluations of actions. But it meant that there were some actions that could not be contemplated, no matter how desirable the likely outcome. The end, in short, did not justify the means.

An important feature of Christian morality, while the pre-Enlightenment consensus lasted, was the principle of double effect. This states that if an act, not evil in itself, has both good and bad effects, provided that the evil effect is not intended, the good effect is not produced by means of the bad effect, and the good achieved outweighs on balance the harm done. The principle of double effect has been much derided by consequentialists; and indeed for a utilitarian, since there are no absolutely forbidden kinds of act, and every deed is to be judged in relation to its consequences, the principle would have no application. Hence many contemporary philosophers regard the principle as at best a Catholic quirk, at worst a sophistical form of double-speak.

On the contrary, I believe that a principle of double effect must form part of any rational system of morality, and it has many everyday applications. There are cases where it makes a huge moral difference whether an outcome is intended or merely foreseen. For instance there is nothing wrong with appointing the best person to a job even though you know that by doing so you will give pain to the other candidates. It would be a very different matter if you appointed A (even though the best candidate) for the express purpose of giving pain to B.

Of course there can be sophistical uses of the principle, where somebody simply redescribes an evil action in euphemistic terms, for instance when someone administers a drug in order to shorten a patient's life, while claiming to be merely aiming at reducing pain. But there is a clear way of sorting out whether a foreseen bad consequence of an action is or is not intended. Suppose that one does, for a good purpose, a lawful act A, which is likely to have bad consequence B. To see whether B is or is not intended, ask whether if, contrary to expectations, B did not happen, would one's purpose be frustrated? If it would not, then the plea that it is unintended may well be valid.

9

Life and Death

The most important moral issues are concerned with the taking of the life of one human being by another. It seems generally agreed in our society that one adult should not, on private authority and in the absence of consent, take the life of another adult. But once we move in any direction from that consensus, controversy may set in. The most serious of such controversies at the present time concern the point at which the protection of the individual life should begin and end. In this chapter I will address these two concerns.

When did I begin? When does any individual human being begin? At what stage of its development does a human organism become entitled to the moral and legal protection which we give to the life of human adults? Is it at conception, or at birth, or somewhere between the two?

The three alternatives – at conception, at birth or between – do not in fact exhaust the possibilities. Plato, and some Jewish and Christian admirers of Plato, thought that individual human persons existed as souls before the conception of the bodies they would eventually inhabit. This idea found expression in the Book of Wisdom, where Solomon says 'I was a boy of happy disposition: I had received a good soul as my lot, or rather, being good, I had entered an undefiled body'. Clement of Alexandria records an early Christian notion that the soul is introduced by an angel into a suitably purified womb. Surely such fantasies have little relevance to any contemporary moral debate.

But in addition to those who thought that the individual soul existed before conception, there have been those who thought that the individual body existed before conception, in the shape of the father's semen. Onan, in Genesis, spilt his seed on the ground; in Jewish tradition this was seen not only as a form of sexual pollution but an offence against life. Aquinas, in the *Summa contra Gentiles*, in a chapter on 'the disordered emission of semen' treats both masturbation and contraception as a crime against humanity, second only to homicide. Such a view is natural in the context of a biological belief that only the male gamete provides the active element in conception, so that the sperm is an early stage of the very same individual as eventually comes to birth. Masturbation is then the same kind of thing, on a minor scale, as the exposure of an infant. The high point of this line of thinking was the Bull *Effraenatam* of Pope Sixtus V (1588), which imposed an excommunication, revocable only by the Pope himself, on all forms of contraception as well as on abortion. But the view that masturbation is a poor man's homicide cannot survive the knowledge that both male and female gametes contribute equally to the genetic constitution of the offspring.

At the other extreme are those who maintain that it is not until some time after birth that human rights arise. In pagan antiquity infanticide was very broadly accepted. No sharp line was drawn between infanticide and abortion, and as a method of population control abortion was sometimes regarded as inferior to infanticide, since it did not distinguish between healthy and unhealthy offspring.

In our own time a number of secular philosophers have been prepared to defend infanticide of severely deformed and disabled children. They have based their position on a theory of personality that, as we have seen in an earlier chapter, goes back to John Locke. Only persons have rights, and not every human being is a person: only one who, as Locke puts it in his *Essay* (II, 27), 'has reason and reflection, and considers itself as itself, the same thinking thing, in different times and different places'. Very young infants clearly do not possess this degree of self-awareness, and hence, it is argued, they are not persons and do not have an inviolable right to life.

Defenders of infanticide are still, mercifully, very few in number. It is more common for moralists to take the rejection of infanticide as a starting point for the evaluation of other positions. Any argument that is used to justify abortion, or IVF, or stem-cell research must undergo the following test: would the same argument justify infanticide? If so, then it must be rejected.

The central issue, then, is to record, and decide between, the three alternatives from which we began: should we take individual human life as beginning at conception, at birth, or at some point in between? If the correct alternative is the third one, then we must ask further questions. What, in the course of pregnancy, is the crucial moment? Is it the point of formation (when the foetus has acquired distinct organs), or is it the point of quickening (when the movements of the foetus are perceptible to the mother)? Can we identify the moment by specifying a number of days from the beginning of pregnancy?

Some familiar texts from the Bible suggest that we should opt for conception as the beginning of the individual life of the person. 'In sin did my mother conceive me' sang the Psalmist (51, 5). Job cursed not only the day on which he was born but also 'the night that said "there is a man-child conceived"' (3, 3). Since 1869 it has been the dominant position among Roman Catholics, but for most of the history of the Catholic Church it was a minority view.

It has been much less common to regard personality and human rights as beginning only at the moment of birth. But one important rabbinic text allows abortion up to, but not including, the time when a child's head has emerged from the womb. Some Stoics seem to have taught that the human soul was received when a baby drew its first breath, just as it departs when a man draws his last breath.

Through most of the history of Western Europe, however, the majority opinion has been that individual human life begins at some time after conception and before birth. In the terminology that for centuries seemed most natural, the 'ensoulment' of the individual could be dated at a certain period after the intercourse that produced the offspring. Among Christian thinkers the general consensus was that the human soul was directly created by God and that it was infused into the embryo when the form of the body was completed, which was generally held to occur around 40 days after conception.

Thomas Aquinas held a particularly complicated version of this consensus position. He did not believe that individual human life began at conception; the developing human foetus, for him, does not count as a human being until it possesses a human soul, and that does not happen until some way into pregnancy. For him the first substance independent of the mother is the embryo living a plant life with a vegetative soul. This vegetable substance disappears and is succeeded by a substance with an animal soul, capable of nutrition and sensation. Only at an advanced stage is the rational soul infused by God, turning this animal into a human being. Early-term abortion, therefore, though immoral on other grounds, was not murder.

The whole process of development, according to Aquinas, is supervised by the father's semen, which he believed to remain present and active throughout the first 40 days of pregnancy. For this biological narrative Aquinas claimed, on slender grounds, the authority of Aristotle. At this distance of time, it is difficult to see why Aquinas's teaching on this topic should be accorded great respect.

A survey of the history of the topic makes it abundantly clear that there is no such thing as *the* Christian consensus on the timing of the origin of the human individual. There was, indeed, a consensus among all denominations until well into the twentieth century that abortion was sinful, and that late abortion was homicide. There was no agreement whether early abortion was homicide. However those who deny that it was still regarded as wrong because it was the destruction of a potential, if not an actual, human individual. There was again no agreement whether the wrongfulness of early abortion carried over into the destruction of semen prior to any conception. Even within the Roman Church, different Popes can be cited in support of each option.

The question whether early abortion is homicide was and is important, because if it is not, then the rights and interests of human beings may legitimately be allowed to override the protection that by common consent should in normal circumstances be extended to the early embryo. The preservation of the life of the mother, the fertilization of otherwise barren couples and the furthering of medical research may all, it may be argued, provide reasons to override the embryo's protected status.

This line of argument was found convincing by the members of the Warnock committee on human fertilization (1984) and later by the Harries committee on stem-cell research (2002). They made a significant contribution to the debate by offering a new *terminus ante quem* for the origin of individual human life – one which was much earlier in pregnancy than the 40 days set by the pre-Reformation Christian consensus. Experimentation on embryos, they thought, should be impermissible after the fourteenth day. The reasons for that conclusion were well summarized in the House of Commons in 1985 by the then Secretary of State for Health, the Rt Hon. Kenneth Clarke.

A cell that will become a human being – an embryo or conceptus – will do so within fourteen days. If it is not implanted within fourteen days it will never have a birth. . . . The basis for the fourteen day limit was that it related to the stage of implantation which I have just described, and to the stage at which it is still uncertain whether an embryo will divide into one or more individuals, and thus up to the stage before true individual development has begun. Up to fourteen days that embryo could become one person, two people, or even more. (Hansard, vol. 73, col. 686)

This ethical reasoning is rejected by those Catholics who insist that individual human life begins at conception. An embryo, from the first moment of its existence, has the potential to become a rational human being, and therefore should be allotted full human rights. To be sure, an embryo cannot think, or reason, or exhibit any of the other activities that define rationality: but neither can a newborn baby. The protection that we afford to infants shows that we accept that it is potentiality, rather than actuality, that determines the conferment of human rights.

Undoubtedly, whatever Aquinas may have thought, there is an uninterrupted history of development linking conception with the eventual life of the adult. However, the line of development from conception to fetal life is not the interrupted history *of an individual*. In its early days, as Kenneth Clarke indicated, a single zygote may turn into something that is not a human being at all, or something that is one human being, or something that is two people or more. Foetus, child and adult have a continuous individual development which gamete and zygote do not have. To count embryos is not the same as to count human beings, and in the case of twinning there will be two different human individuals each of whom will be able to trace their life story back to the same embryo, but neither of whom will be the same individual as that embryo.

Those who argue for conception as the moment of origin stress that before fertilization we have two entities (two different gametes) and after it we have a single one (one zygote). A moment at which one entity (a single embryo) splits into two entities (two identical twins) is surely equally entitled to be regarded as a defining moment. It is true that in the vast majority of cases twinning does not actuallly take place; but surely the strongest element in the Catholic position is the emphasis it places on the ethical importance of potentiality. It is the potentiality of twinning, not its actuality, that gives reason for doubting that an early embryo is an individual human being.

In my view, the balance of the arguments leads us to place the individuation of the human being somewhere around the fourteenth day of pregnancy. But there are two sides to the reasoning that leads to that conclusion. If the course of development of the embryo gives good reason to believe that before the fourteenth day it is not an individual human being, it gives equally good reason to believe that after that time it *is* an individual human being. If so, then late abortion is indeed homicide – and abortion becomes 'late' at an earlier date than was ever dreamt of by Aquinas.

Since most abortion in practice takes place well after the stage at which the embryo has become an individual human being, it may seem that the philosophical and theological argument about the moment of ensoulment has little practical moral relevance. That is not so. If the life of an individual human being begins at conception, then all practices which involve the deliberate destruction of embryos, at whatever stage, deserve condemnation. That is why there has been official Catholic opposition to various forms of IVF and to scientific research involving stem cells. But if the embryo, in its earliest days, is not yet an individual human being, then it need not necessarily be immoral to sacrifice it to the greater good of actual human beings who wish to conceive a child or reap the benefits of medical research.

I turn now from the question of the inception of human life (and its extinction at pre-natal stage) to the issues surrounding its termination by human agency. The next chapter will be concerned with the taking of life in warfare and warlike situations; in the present chapter I consider the morality of peacetime killing, whether in the form of capital punishment, euthanasia or suicide.

That the state has the right to take the life of one of its citizens as a punishment for crime was until the last century accepted by most Christian theologians, including Aquinas. This is a teaching that even some of his most devoted followers find difficult to accept, claiming that it is a violation of the principle that one may not do evil that good may come. But anyone who is not a pacifist must accept that the deliberate taking of human life may sometimes be lawful. If a national community may in a just war lawfully take the life of citizens of other states, it is hard to see why it is absolutely prohibited from taking the life of one of its own citizens. To be sure, human life has a value greater than any human property, so if capital punishment is to be justified it must be used only as a punishment for murder, and not for lesser crimes such as theft.

The strongest argument against capital punishment is that, given the fallibility of judges and juries, it is inevitable that from time to time innocent people will be wrongly executed. The strongest argument in favour of capital punishment, is that without it society has no further sanction against further taking of life by murderers who are already serving life sentences in prison. It would be possible to do justice to both arguments by a legal system that allowed the death penalty to be imposed only after the second of two convictions for murder.

Campaigners for human rights commonly oppose the death penalty for offenders, but some of them believe that the state should permit the taking of an innocent human being's life if it has become intolerable. In most countries at present euthanasia and assisted suicide are illegal, and there are many ethical and legal problems that surround any hastening of the moment of death.

When we try to distinguish cases where it is, and where it is not, morally permissible to cause the death of oneself or of another we see the importance of the differences between the moral systems that were outlined in the previous chapter. For a utilitarian, whatever the legal system in force, it can in principle be morally legitimate deliberately to kill a patient whose suffering has become unbearable and who wishes to die. Many Christians, however, believe that it is never permissible, either for a public authority or a private citizen, deliberately to take the life of an innocent person, even at their own request.

It is at this point that the principle of double effect – discussed in the previous chapter – can come into play. The principle states that it may be legitimate to bring about unintentionally a state of affairs which it would be immoral to bring about deliberately. Thus, while it is wrong to give a lethal dose of a drug in order to terminate life, it may be acceptable to give, in order to relieve suffering, a dose of a painkiller which will, in fact, shorten the patient's life.

The principle of double effect is often criticized by utilitarian moralists, but in everyday life we readily accept that there is an important moral difference between aiming at a particular outcome and bringing about the same outcome without aiming at it. It is unfriendly deliberately to seat a guest at table next to a person she dislikes; it is not unfriendly if the assignment is the unavoidable outcome of the conventions of placement. It seems to me not at all unreasonable to accept the application of the principle of double effect even to matters of life and death.

Some Christian moralists go further and are willing to allow that the intentional killing of an innocent human being may in principle be morally permissible. This is when a patient lacks the possibility of responsible life because permanently bereft of the physical preconditions of consciousness, or because of intense and irremediable suffering. A person's biological life, it is sometimes said, may persist while her biographical life has come to an end.

One need not be sceptical about the ability of the medical profession to make reliable predictions about permanent vegetative states in order to oppose the legalization of the termination of life in such cases. Any legalization of euthanasia is likely to lead in practice to the toleration of forms of killing that should only be treated as murder. There are not one but two slippery slopes to be avoided. One leads from authorizing a doctor to kill a patient at the patient's request to authorizing a doctor to kill whenever he himself judges that the patient would be better off dead. The other leads from authorization to kill a patient in intolerable agony to authorization to kill a patient who has lost interest in life. Legal decisions in the Netherlands, since euthanasia was legalized there in 1984, show that such slippery slopes are not fictions of the imagination.

What are we to say of suicide? Religious believers may say, with Socrates, that we are God's cattle and our lives belong to Him and not to ourselves, or they may say with Thomas More that we should not seek to go to God before he calls us. On the other hand, the ancient Stoics taught that 'the wise man may reasonably make his own exit from life, for the sake of his country or dear ones, or if he suffer intolerable pain, handicap, or disease'. Many people at the present time admire this Stoic teaching and regard suicide as justifiable in the circumstances it describes. They forget, perhaps, that for the Stoics it was almost impossible to find a wise man, and it was only he who was authorized to kill himself.

In discussing the pros and cons of euthanasia and suicide it is impossible to avoid citing one's own experience. My mother died at the age of 99; until the last days of her life she was in full possession of her mental faculties though afflicted in other ways and often in considerable pain. She had become a burden to herself and others and said many times that her life had been too long and that she wished to die. Throughout her last years I was constantly grateful that the law forbade euthanasia and that my mother's Catholic principles prevented her from ever considering suicide. I can think of few things worse than to have to take part in a decision deliberately to terminate the life of a parent, and I am thankful that I was never called upon to do so.

In a long life I have been close to a number of people who ended their own lives. In each case, the grief and misery caused to others appeared to me greatly to outweigh – even on the crudest utilitarian calculation – the relief from the sufferings that caused them to take such a step. I can only hope that I will never be subject to the temptation they underwent, and pray that if I do I will be given the strength to resist it.

I end this chapter on an even more personal note, by describing the last years of a friend who met his death in a manner that I would be happy to take as a model, namely Norman Kreztmann, who taught for most of his professional life at Cornell University in upstate New York. Kreztmann was brought up a Lutheran, and descended from a long line of Lutheran pastors going back to the age of Luther himself. But he lost his Lutheran faith at university and for most of his life was an atheist. A few years before his death he seems to have recovered a belief in the existence of God, but it was a philosophical belief that did not involve adherence to any Church, nor, I think, any hope of an afterlife.

Kretzmann devoted most of his teaching to medieval philosophy – initially to the logic of the late Middle Ages. About a decade before his death he began to take a profound interest in the study of Thomas Aquinas, and undertook a critical commentary on the *Summa contra Gentiles*. Three years after the commencement of this work he was diagnosed as suffering from a lethal cancer – multiple myeloma. The doctors gave him a year to live. In fact, he survived for a further seven years, and up to the last days of his life he continued to work on his commentary. Two volumes were completed and published by OUP, and a substantial part of a third remained unpublished at his death: the published volumes were entitled *The Metaphysics of Theism* (1997) and *The Metaphysics of Creation* (1999). The work is of a high standard, and would do great credit to a man in perfect health.

A few weeks before his death, while talking to him on the telephone, I congratulated him on his stoical attitude while under sentence of death. 'You are treating your illness very philosophically', I said. 'Of course', he replied, 'I have a PhD in that subject.'

10

The Individual, the State and the Globe

Patriotism is a virtue. A century ago that is something that would have gone without saying. The memorials to the dead of two World Wars that stand in every town and village witness to an era in which the willingness to sacrifice one's life for one's country was seen as the supreme form of human heroism. But partly because of the immensity of the slaughter involved in those two wars, in the latter half of the twentieth century many people came to regard patriotism as, if not actually a vice, at least a highly suspect virtue. Many a writer quoted – with approval but without context – Samuel Johnson's dictum 'Patriotism is the last refuge of a scoundrel'.

But patriotism remains a necessity, though its forms may change. It is a great benefit to human beings to live in societies organized into states, as we can see as soon as we look at the poverty, insecurity and horror that is the lot of those who live in 'failed states'. When the stability of government is threatened by external or internal violence, it is important that there should be military and police forces to protect it. For most of us, the form that patriotism takes in practice is the willingness to pay the taxes that underpin the workings of the state. But a nation of taxpayers without any soldiers or policemen would not have a long expectation of life. So we can be grateful that there remain those who patriotism extends to their acceptance of risk to life and limb in the service of their country.

But patriotism that takes a coldly economic form is a dismal virtue. It is good to take a pride in one's country and to be concerned about its reputation. It is no bad thing to rejoice in the triumphs of national sportsmen, and to feel embarrassed when their fans misbehave. It is good to rejoice in the victories of our armed services, if they are engaged in a just war, and it is right to feel shame when members of our forces commit war crimes. If one lives in a country with independent and uncorrupt courts and a tradition of hospitality to refugees and immigrants, it is right to take pride in these things, and to worry about any threat to them.

But though patriotism is a necessary virtue, its dictates are not absolute; they must be qualified by other values if patriotism is not to decay into xenophobia. We should remember, not Johnson's apophthegm but Edith Cavell's words on the eve of her execution in 1915. 'Standing as I do in view of God and eternity, I realize that patriotism is not enough.'

I find Cavell's words truer than ever at a time when my country is a member of a larger community – the European Union – and when all countries are members of the United Nations and are increasingly part of a single global culture and economy. I wish now to consider each of these communities in turn.

The first book I ever read about the concept of Europe was by the English Catholic historian Hilaire Belloc. It was called *Europe and the Faith*. It had a simple theme: the essence of Europe was the Catholic faith, and the Catholic Church was the continuation of the Roman Empire. Belloc pointed out that the nations which had broken away from Rome at the Reformation had either, like Germany and Scotland, never been parts of the ancient Roman Empire or, like England and the countries north of the Danube had been, as Roman provinces, late-comers and early-leavers. Even as a Catholic schoolboy I noticed that there was a slight problem with Belloc's identification of the Faith with the Europe of the Roman Empire. The two most devout Catholic countries, Ireland and Poland, had never been parts of the Empire and were even further removed from its boundaries than the Nordic countries that had accepted the Reformation. Belloc, of course, was aware of this difficulty. He offered various implausible explanations to show that these exceptions did not disprove his rule.

Belloc was right that any attempt to characterize the common features that bind together the peoples of

Europe is bound to trace their history back to the Roman Empire. The history of Europe can indeed be seen as passing through four stages, of which the first was that imperial period. The second was the age of Christendom. The third was the period of the European nation states. The fourth was the period since the Second World War of the association between states that produced the European Union whose constitution still awaits definition.

There are several characteristics that separate the first phase from its successors. There are obvious geographical differences between the Roman Empire and the European Union. Much of the European Union – particularly since its recent enlargement – was outside the boundaries of the Roman Empire at its widest extent. More importantly, much of the Roman Empire lay outside anything we nowadays think of as European. The Empire was a Mediterranean empire, and included North Africa, Egypt and the Middle East.

The Roman Empire differed from the modern Europe of nation states in that it was unified under a single authority. This authority had, for the most part, been imposed by force, but it was maintained with a comparatively gentle hand. For several centuries, between the frontier of Rhine and Danube and the edges of the Maghreb, from Gibraltar to Palmyra, peace reigned, with brief and comparatively trivial interruptions, and culture and commerce thrived under a uniform system of law. It is true that in medieval Christendom, too, the whole of Europe fell within the bounds of a universal jurisdiction; but that authority was never as effective as the Roman Imperium had been in enforcing stability and tranquillity, and in the Middle Ages the price of cohesion was religious uniformity. In the Roman Empire, on the other hand, despite the spasmodic persecution of Christians, religious toleration was the general rule.

After the Empire fell into decay, there followed centuries in which there was no entity which could be considered as Europe. In East and West, survivors of the lost glory clung to fragments of tradition. In Constantinople a shrivelled remnant was preserved of imperial power and classical culture, while in Italy, as Thomas Hobbes memorably remarked, the Papacy was no more than a ghost sitting crowned upon the Empire's grave. When the European idea revived, its next incarnation was born out of the fight for survival against the engulfing tide of Muslim invasion.

Within a century of the death of the prophet Muhammad in 633 the religion of Islam had spread by conquest from its native Arabia throughout the neighbouring Persian Empire and the Roman provinces of North Africa; their advance, across Spain and into Northern Europe, was halted only in 732 when they were defeated at Tours, near Poitiers, by the Frankish leader Charles Martel.

Charlemagne, Charles Martel's grandson, who became King of the Franks in 768, drove the Muslims back into the Pyrenees, but did no more than nibble at their Spanish dominions. His military and political ambitions for France were more concerned with its eastern frontier. He conquered Lombardy, Bavaria and Saxony and had his son proclaimed King of Italy. After rescuing Pope Leo III from a revolution in Rome he was himself crowned Roman Emperor in St Peter's on Christmas Day 800. By the time of his death in 814 almost all the Christian inhabitants of continental Western Europe were united under his rule.

The coronation of 800 was the beginning of the medieval European Empire, though it was not until the twelfth century that it acquired the name of Holy Roman Empire. It is to Charlemagne and his successors that we owe one of the most important ideas in the history of Europe: the idea that national political power should be limited, with reference to some transnational eternal yardstick. Of course, during the high Middle Ages there was not one, there were two supranational authorities. The Papacy and the Empire did not always exhibit the harmony that Charlemagne and Leo displayed when the former was crowned by the latter. Often the two institutions clashed like any other pair of superpowers. But this second period of the European ideal survived until the early sixteenth century, when another Charles and another Leo tried, vainly, to preserve the unity of Christendom against the Lutheran revolution.

When Sir Thomas More was condemned to death for his refusal to swear to an Act of Henry VIII derogating from Papal authority, he appealed to the medieval transnational ideal. 'I am not bound, my lord', he told the Lord Chancellor at his trial, 'to conform my conscience to the Council of one Realm against the general council of Christendom.' But when More spoke the ideal of Christendom was already dead. The sack of Papal Rome by imperial troops in 1527 sounded its deathknell.

The division of Christendom was an unnecessary tragedy. The theological issues which separated Luther and Calvin from their Catholic opponents had been debated many times in the Middle Ages without leading to sectarian warfare; and few twentieth-century Catholics and Protestants, if not professionally trained in theology, are aware of the real nature of the differences between the contrasting theories of the Eucharist, of Grace and of Predestination which in the sixteenth century led to anathema and bloodshed.

Questions of authority, of course, are easier to understand and more difficult to arbitrate than questions of doctrine. But the unity of Christendom could have been maintained under a constitutional Papacy subject to general councils, such as Ockham had suggested, such as had been the practice in the fifteenth century,

113

and such as even Thomas More, for the greater part of his life, believed to be the divine design for the Church.

But of course it was not theology that was the predominant force in the break-up of Europe's religious unity. Rather, it was the ambition and avarice of kings and popes, and the growth of nationalist feeling resentful of international control. Feudal loyalties were replaced by loyalties to absolute national sovereigns. The cultural divisions between nations were emphasized as Latin, as a universal language of law and learning, gave way to the growth of local vernacular codes and literatures. By itself, of course, the linguistic developments need not have led to religious struggles. As Charles V said in the synod of Frankfurt: 'Let nobody believe that God can only be prayed to in the three languages [Hebrew, Greek and Latin] because God can be adored and man listened to in every language if what he asks is just'.

But Charles's hope of a unified but multilingual Christendom was a chimera. He was the last Emperor who had truly European authority – and that authority was personal to him and did not pass on to his successors. Henceforth the Holy Roman Empire was a Germanic entity only. In Rome the Papacy dwindled, worn out by its own excesses; for centuries it found it difficult to exert even spiritual authority in the most Catholic countries such as France and Spain. The last reference in an official document to a Res Publica

Christiana is in the Treaty of Utrecht in 1713. The Europe which some statesmen tried to recreate after the Second World War was to be a resurrection of this unified community – whether religious or secular in inspiration is still a matter of urgent controversy.

During the modern period Europe was as much a common battlefield as a common culture. The history of Europe between 1648 and 1945 is in great part a history of wars between European nation states – wars whose operation, if directed from Europe, often spilled over into other continents. At the end of one of the worst of these wars, in 1946, T. S. Eliot, in a broadcast talk to Germany, asked whether, in spite of all this, there were certain common features which made it possible to speak of a European culture. He replied,

> The dominant force in creating a common culture between peoples each of which has its distinct culture, is religion . . . I am not so much concerned with the communion of Christian believers today; I am talking about the common tradition of Christianity which has made Europe what it is, and about the common cultural elements which this common Christianity has brought with it. If Asia were converted to Christianity tomorrow, it would not thereby become a part of Europe. It is in Christianity that our arts have developed; it is in Christianity that the laws of Europe have been

rooted. It is against a background of Christianity that all our thought has significance. An individual European may not believe that the Christian Faith is true, and yet what he says, and makes, and does, will all spring out of his heritage of Christian culture and depend upon that culture for its meaning. Only a Christian culture could have produced a Voltaire or a Nietzsche.

The unity of culture, in contrast to the unity of political organization, does not require us all to have only one loyalty: it means that there will be a variety of loyalties . . . I will give one instance. No university ought to be merely a national institution, even if it is supported by the nation. The universities of Europe should have their common ideals, they should have their obligations towards each other. They should be independent of the governments of the countries in which they are situated. They should not be institutions for the training of an efficient bureaucracy, or for equipping scientists to get the better of foreign scientists; they should stand for the preservation of learning, for the pursuit of truth, and in so far as men are capable of it, the attainment of wisdom. (*Notes towards the Definition of Culture*, p. 122)

This is very well said; but now, 60 years on, Eliot's words need many modifications. What he says about the values common to the countries of Europe applies with equal force to Australia and New Zealand and to America, North and South. The countries of continental Europe are no longer homogeneously Christian or ex-Christian. Many of them house large Muslim communities – reciprocating, one would like to think, the tolerance of Muslim Spain in the medieval period.

In the imperial era Augustus, Claudius and Marcus Aurelius united Europe essentially by force. In the modern era Napoleon tried to do likewise and failed. The fragile medieval unity was based on non-natural premises and religious sanctions. Those who created such political unity as now exists in Europe built it upon the foundation of democratically elected governments of free nations. The first stage was the European Coal and Steel Community of 1952; it was no accident that this first step towards unity concerned the materials crucial to the manufacture of weapons of war. The Treaty of Rome of 1957, which established the EEC, enshrined the objective of 'ever closer union between the peoples of Europe'. By instituting the European Court of Justice it reintroduced the medieval concept of a legal authority higher than any national jurisdiction.

During the build-up of European unity we have now had the longest period of continuous peace between France and Germany ever since those nations came into existence. Looking back, we can see that in the history of the continent the modern Europe of the nation states is the aberration. The task which faces our generation is to combine, in this fourth contemporary stage of European history, the best elements of the previous three – the peaceful religious tolerance of the Roman Empire; the supranational appeal courts of Christendom; the powerful vernacular cultures of the modern age.

But the European Union and its members form only a small portion of the human race that is spread across the globe in a variety of cultures and jurisdictions. The United Nations, born like the European community in the aftermath of the Second World War, is the ultimate transnational entity that has a claim in competition with that of local national patriotism. In a later chapter I argue that in matters of peace and war, the United Nations should be regarded as the sole legitimate authority for the conduct of wars, with the exception of wars of self-defence by a nation attacked by an aggressor state. I look forward to the eventual recognition, by all nations, of an international criminal court to adjudicate upon allegations of war crimes. I regard organs of the United Nations as the most appropriate forums for the determination of transnational issues such as climate change and the terms of international trade. But in this chapter I wish to focus more on two specific matters, not within the competence of any UN body, which are the consequences of increased communication between the members of the world-wide community.

The first is the emergence of English as an international language. The globalization of English is manifest in several ways. First, it is a corollary of the globalization of commerce, given that English is the predominant language of contracts, and of marketing. Second, since one of the most significant commodities for sale on the global market is intellectual property, and since English has become the predominant medium of scientific research, texts in English are the major commodity traded on this market. Finally, the English language itself has become a very profitable commodity to trade; academic publishers earn much greater revenues from textbooks teaching English as a foreign language than from their mainline academic output.

Many see the globalization of English as a marvellous benefit to communication. Some people believe that in an ideal world there would be only one single language, and this would guarantee mutual understanding, enlightenment and peace. At a more mundane level, it is a marvellous boon for Anglophone tourists to be understood everywhere in the world except when ordering a meal in London or directing a taxi in Manhattan. If there is to be a universal language, there is no doubt that English is richer and more flexible than Esperanto or any other artificial language. The present multiplicity of languages – maybe 6,000 of them – are regarded by many people as an expensive and unnecessary luxury for a world community.

I have some sympathy with this rather brutalistic view. I don't take the contrasting view that the death of any existing language is an irretrievable tragedy for the human race. I accept that linguistic diversity is necessary no less than ecological diversity – but I question whether for an adequate linguistic diversity we need all the existing 6,000, just as I question whether every single animal and plant species must be preserved to give us adequate ecological diversity. Every one of us, of course, has a great deal to learn by reading the literature of other cultures in other languages – but a language need not be currently spoken for non-native speakers to enjoy and learn from it. Homer is still one of the most educative and delightful authors to read. So I am unconvinced that the globalization of English threatens us with a doomsday scenario of universal language death. But there is no doubt that the expansion of English as a means of global communication has a very significant downside, and I will mention just three negative aspects of its globalization.

First, the English that is an international language is American English. I don't object to this either on patriotic or linguistic grounds – I think American English is more lively than current British English, and often less sloppy. The problem with American English as a global language is that it is the language of the world's dominating power. Latin as the language of learned communication survived the decline of dominance of the Catholic Church. When in the seventeenth and eighteenth centuries, scholars in England, France and Germany communicated with each other in Latin, this was not the privileging of the vernacular of any nation state.

Second, the Anglicization of intellectual property leads to an enormous global imbalance of intellectual talent; it adds an inequality in human resources to the many other unfairnesses of the global terms of trade. It is not only that the English language is a commodity that has been globalized, but also Anglophone academics, researchers and experts. I am an old-fashioned believer in the international republic of letters and I am proud to be a member of a community of scholars that is a world community. I don't think frontiers should count in science, and when my colleagues, or the British media, deplore the brain drain from Britain to America, my first reaction is to think: if A and B are doing good research, what does it matter to science where they are doing it? If it is only in the United States they can be appropriately recompensed, and get adequate funds for their experiments, then good luck to them. What is sad, though, is that the effect of the brain drain is that the international republic of letters is becoming a national republic of letters; and science for the world is to an ever-greater extent applied science for the United States.

Finally, I believe that even those of us who are native English speakers should give only a highly qualified welcome to the globalization of English. Because of the possibility of speaking English wherever you go anglophones, even if they wish to learn about other peoples, have little incentive to learn other languages. According to English newspapers, polls taken shortly after the tragedy of 9/11 showed that only a small proportion of the US population had any clear idea where Afghanistan was located; and unkind commentators said that war was God's way of teaching Americans geography. Only slightly less unfairly, one might say that intelligence gathering has been God's way of teaching Americans foreign languages. With the decline of interest in intelligence after the end of the Cold War, enthusiasm for learning difficult languages declined. I have seen it reported that throughout the class of 2001 in the whole of America there were only seven people who took bachelors degrees in Arabic. We in Britain have no reason to imagine ourselves superior to the US in our ability to master other languages, and the present British government has reduced the already minimal requirements for language learning in schools.

One final reason, therefore, why I hesitate to welcome wholeheartedly the globalization of English is because of its effect on those like myself whose mother tongue is English. To bowdlerize Rudyard Kipling, 'What do they know of English who only English know?' I went myself to a very old-fashioned school and the way I learnt to appreciate the structure, power and flexibility of English was by learning to translate into and out of Latin and ancient Greek. These two, I accept, are not the most useful languages for the purposes of tourism or counter-terrorism intelligence: but the learning of classical languages was a marvellous introduction to the appreciation of cultures distant in space and time, which is one of the most precious of transferable skills. Moreover it provided a template for the learning of foreign languages of more obvious utility, and for the comparative study of the incomparable treasures of the English language itself.

In the final part of this chapter I want to draw attention to an unintended effect of the recent global expansion of technology. Globalization, I want to argue, of its nature tends to make us all more selfish. The argument is in essence simple. Power, we all know, corrupts. Technology gives power, therefore technology corrupts. It does so not just by giving us power to do evil (for instance, to destroy the world with nuclear weapons), but by giving us the power to do good (for instance, the power to put clean water within the reach of the entire human race). It puts sins of omission as immediately and inevitably within our power as it puts sins of commission.

Let me spell out the argument more soberly. We are surely responsible for evils we know about and can prevent or remedy without disproportionate loss. As technology increases our knowledge of evils and our power to remove them, it increases our responsibility for not removing them. It makes it more and more likely that we will be selfish.

We might take as a simple and crude measure of self-ishness, in contrast to altruism, the amount of one's time, energy, money and power that one devotes to the satisfaction of one's own needs and desires by compari-son with the amount of time that one devotes to the satisfaction of the needs and desires of others. Let us consider an average selfish man ('*l'homme moyen egoiste*'). Let us suppose that he devotes half his resources, half his time, money, energy and power, to himself, and half his resources to others.

In a primitive society this average selfish man is free from blame. It takes, let us say, half his working life to produce enough to support himself, and he devotes to his fellow humans all the time that he has to spare from keeping himself alive – and if those fellow humans are his wife and family, that's fine. He is not responsible for any human suffering because there is none that he can remedy without imperilling his own life – something that may be estimable and heroic to do, but which is not normally obligatory to do.

But let us remember the process, to which Marx drew

attention, by which, as technology advances, less and less of our working life is devoted to actually providing ourselves with food, warmth and clothes. Many people in developed countries today have an income more than twenty times as much as is necessary to keep them at subsistence level. Such a person, therefore, before the end of the first working day, has earned enough to keep herself or himself alive for the week. What, in these circumstances, is the moral situation of average selfish persons? They show up very poorly. They need only to devote 5 per cent of their income to keeping themselves alive, and in fact they devote 50 per cent of their income to the satisfaction of their own desires. Their lifestyle expresses a preference for superfluities for themselves above subsistence for others. They must bear some responsibility for the amount of suffering that could have been prevented by their allocation of the extra 45 per cent of their resources to altruistic purposes.

The argument I have just given is one that occurred to me many years ago. It is obviously very crude, and needs refinement in many ways. I have not, however, been able to detect a fundamental flaw in it. I fervently hope that there is one, because if not it means that the world is bound to become more and more corrupt unless altruism increases *pari passu* with science and the technological power it gives, of which I see no likelihood. Moreover, I must confess that I have never myself given to the poorest of the world a sufficient amount of my income even to compete with my imaginary average selfish man.

11

War

In its origins, Christianity was a pacifist religion. Jesus'
teaching emphasized non-violence, non-resistance and
non-retaliation. Not until three centuries later, when
the Roman Emperors were converted, was it generally
agreed to be proper for a Christian to become a soldier.
Not until the time of Augustine was there anything
that could be called a Christian theory of military
ethics. However, by the sixteenth century theologians
had developed a systematic theory of justice in warfare.
The most eloquent exponents of the just war tradition
were Francisco Suarez on the Catholic side and Hugo
Grotius on the Protestant side. If one leaves on one side
the international role of the Papacy, the teaching of the
two men was remarkably similar, and it remains the
basis of the international law of war to this day. It may
be summed up as follows.

A war may only be conducted by a legitimate authority, not by private citizens. A war may only be waged in
order to right or avert a specific wrong: that is what

gives the right to go to war, the *ius ad bellum*. War should be taken up only as a last resort when other measures of redressing the grievance or preventing aggression have failed. There must be good hope of victory, and the good to be obtained by the righting of the wrong must outweigh the harm which will be done by the choice of war as a means. Finally, one must observe certain rules in the actual conduct of the war: that is justice in war itself, the *ius in bello*. The deliberate killing of non-combatants and the ill-treatment of prisoners will render unjust a war which may initially have begun with solid justification.

The condition of lawful authority has commonly been interpreted as meaning that wars may be waged only by sovereign governments. It is generally agreed that individuals and groups within a state have no right to settle their differences by force of arms. More contentious is the role of supranational bodies, such as the Papacy in the sixteenth century and the United Nations in our own.

Individual nations have the right, both in ethics and in international law, to take up arms to defend themselves when attacked, or manifestly about to be attacked, by a hostile state. But can it also be legitimate to wage an offensive war: to attack another state if that is the only way to remedy a grave injustice to oneself or one's allies, or even to secure, within the hostile state itself, a change of regime for the better? At the present time, in my view, such an attack can only be legitimate if authorized by the United Nations.

The second condition has several elements. Before beginning war, a sovereign must offer the potential enemy the opportunity to remedy the evil complained of. Only if he fails to do so may he be attacked. Hostilities may be initiated only if there is good hope of victory: otherwise the recourse to arms will fail to remedy the injustice which provided the initial ground for war. In the course of the war, only such violence must be used as is necessary to achieve victory. After the war, compensation may be exacted, and wartime wrongdoers may be punished.

The requirement of *ius in bello* was traditionally formulated as a prohibition on the killing of the innocent, but the innocence in question had nothing to do with moral guiltlessness or lack of responsibility. The 'innocent' were those who were not *nocentes*, not engaged in harming your side. Soldiers who had surrendered were, in this sense, no less 'innocent' than infants in arms and had an equal right to be spared. The traditional principle is best formulated thus: it is lawful to kill only those who are engaged in waging war or supplying those who are waging war with the means of doing so.

The principle, thus formulated, does justify the deliberate killing of more than those who are wearing uniform. It regards as justified, for instance, the killing of munitions workers, or of civilians driving military transports. Moreover, the principle accepts that it is likely in war that civilians will die as a collateral effect of attacks on military targets. Once more the principle of double effect comes into play, and such deaths need not necessarily count as murderous. The number of unintended deaths, however, is obviously relevant to the question whether a war is doing more harm than good. What was absolutely ruled out by the principles of *ius in bello* was the deliberate massacre of civilian populations or the devastation of whole cities, whether as an end in itself or as a means to victory.

Just war theory was, as I have said, developed by Christian theologians, but there is nothing in their arguments that appeals to especially Christian premises, and several of the rules laid down have been embodied from time to time in international agreements. The rules are not a set of arbitrary prohibitions, but an articulation of the only conditions under which the international community can rationally accept war. War is justifiable only if war can be limited, just as within an individual society police forces are necessary but are tolerable only if there are limits on police powers.

The theory of the just war stands opposed to two other ethical attitudes to war. On the one hand, there is the pacificist view that no war, however limited, can ever be justified. On the other hand, there are those who believe that there can be holy wars in which the sanctity of the war aims will justify the killing of enemy non-combatants. Both Christians and Muslims have from time to time declared holy wars – crusades, on the one hand, and *jihads* on the other.

The rules of just war theory were, however, framed in the context of symmetrical wars, wars between nation states of approximately equal power. How far does just war theory need adaptation when applied to the asymmetrical wars which have become more frequent in recent years? Perhaps the most common asymmetrical war is one between a nation and an armed group within it that is less than a nation. We may put the question: Can there be a just rebellion as there can be a just war – and if so, what are the conditions under which it can be waged?

Given that the first condition for a just war is that it be waged by legitimate authority, it may seem that bearing arms against a government can never be justified. But that is to ignore the possibility that a government may behave so badly as to forfeit all claim to legitimacy. Such a loss of authority on the part of the government is one half of the first condition for just rebellion. The other half is that the rebelling group should be in a position, if victorious, to set up an alternative government with popular consent. One of the reasons for authority being the first condition for just war is that there should be a focus of command in each

131

of the warring powers: otherwise there can be no possibility of a negotiation to end the war. Thus, it is similarly important – for moral as well as political reasons – that there should be a disciplined chain of command among rebellious forces.

The other conditions for a just war – proportionality, hope of victory, last resort – apply without significant alteration when we are considering just rebellion. The condition of non-combatant immunity, also, remains in force; but there is scope for a modification in the definition of 'combatant'. In a war between nations, the civil police are not legitimate targets, as they are not engaged in military combat. However, in a rebellion against an intolerable government, it may well be argued that police may be targeted since they are the key agents of the repression that justifies the uprising.

The targeting of non-combatants is what turns rebellion into terrorism. If we leave aside what is misleadingly called 'state terrorism', the most common form of terrorism can be defined as rebellion that does not observe the conditions of just rebellion. The distinction between just and unjust rebellion is not a piece of academic pedantry: the definition of legitimate targets during a rebellion has been a serious issue in many liberation movements. This was the issue which caused a split between the Official and the Provisional IRA in Northern Ireland; and it was a topic of keen debate, as recorded in Nelson Mandela's autobiography, within the ANC and its military wing MS in South Africa.

At the present time, wars between nations seem to many people to threaten peace less than the activities of terrorist groups within states and a potential clash of civilizations with different religious traditions. There is, however, no such thing as 'a war against terrorism': terrorism, it has justly been said, is not an enemy but a tactic. The use of the phrase, if it is not mere rhetoric, is a cloak for the removal of the constraints which due process imposes when murderers are dealt with by the criminal law. Talk of the clash of civilizations obscures the fact that with respect to the rules of combat main-stream Muslims and moderate Christians share a common tradition.

In its early years Islam was a much more warlike religion than Christianity was in its origins. In the very first year of the Hegira Muhammad authorized war to redress the wrongs that Muslims had suffered in Mecca, and within a century of his death Islam had spread by conquest from Arabia throughout the neighbouring Persian Empire, the whole of North Africa and most of Spain. However, by the time of the major wars between Christian and Muslim – the Crusades in the East, the Reconquista in Spain and the Ottoman invasion of southern and central Europe – Muslim theologians had worked out a theoretical structure for the ethics of warfare which was not altogether different from the

Christian one. They reflected upon the legitimacy of achieving military objectives by methods which entailed heavy civilian casualties. They debated, for instance, whether it was lawful to use a mangonel against a besieged city, since it would kill women and children as well as soldiers. The predominant tradition in Muslim theology would undoubtedly condemn the suicide bombings of the present day.

However, while moralists in both faiths have sought to restrain the resort to war, and to check cruelty and brutality in the conduct of war the majority of wars actually fought, whether by Christians or Muslims, have been unjust wars unjustly waged. Holy wars, in which protagonists feel that the lofty nature of their motives justifies disdain for mere humanity or decency, are the worst of all wars. The medieval Christian theory of war was probably more humane than the Islamic theory. But in practice the Crusaders more than matched any of their enemies in brutal ferocity. Salah-al-Din's generous treatment of the inhabitants of Jerusalem when he recaptured it in 1187 was in marked contrast to the bloodbath there that marked the successful end of the First Crusade a hundred years earlier. But even the atrocities of 1099 paled by comparison with those inflicted on their fellow Christians by the knights of the Fourth Crusade after the sack of Constantinople in 1204.

12

Sex

Of the philosophical clichés of the last century, one of the silliest was the slogan 'you can't derive an ought from an is': a normative conclusion could never be derived from factual premises. It is true that the fact that something is the case does not entail that it ought to be the case, any more than the fact that something ought to be the case entails that it is the case. But it is absurd to suggest that factual information is irrelevant to moral judgement. Nowhere is such a suggestion more inappropriate than in the case of sexual ethics. Biological information about the natural processes of human reproduction, and the technological possibilities of artificial control of those processes are both matters of fact that have to be taken into account in any rational system of sexual ethics.

A society which was unaware of the connection between copulation and procreation would surely have a sexual ethic very different from that of any civilized society; and reasonably so. A society of that kind can easily be imagined, and there appear to be historical examples of such societies. It is much harder to imagine a human society whose members were unaware of the connection between eating and drinking, on the one hand, and the health and life of the individual on the other. Hunger, thirst and sex are universally dominant human appetites, but the third differs from the first two in being biologically directed not to the survival of the individual but to the survival of the species. For this reason moral agents find it much easier to identify with the biological purpose of the first two appetites than with the biological purpose of the third.

In the case of sex there can be no simple identification of the biologically effective with the morally obligatory. Christians in many ages have urged that since the biological purpose of sex is procreation it is a sin against the author of nature to indulge in non-procreative sex. This principle, however it may have been qualified over the ages, underpins the Catholic Church's opposition to contraception – though in recent times, with the development of IVF and artificial forms of human reproduction, the emphasis of ecclesiastical concern seems to have shifted from 'No copulation without procreation' to 'No procreation without copulation'.

History shows, however, that no society has ever been able to enforce, or even consistently maintain, the moral principle that the only worthy motive for sex is the desire to procreate. In the ancient world, the first moralist to base sexual morality on the notion that procreation is the natural purpose of sex was Plato in his late work *The Laws*. At one point in that dialogue the leading character says that he would like to put into effect 'a law to permit sexual intercourse only for its natural purpose, procreation, and to prohibit homosexual relations; to forbid the deliberate killing of a human offspring and the casting of seed on rocks and stone where it will never take root and fructify' (8, 838e). Such a law, however, would be very difficult to enforce, and instead the dialogue proposes other measures to stamp out sodomy and discourage other forms of non-procreative intercourse. The heterosexual puritanism of the *Laws* comes oddly from a writer whose better known dialogues are full of arch homosexual banter and portray a colourful gay culture; but the sentiments it enshrines were to be influential throughout much of the Christian centuries.

Modern Christians in discussing sexual activity, and more generally social relations between the sexes, often refer (with approval or dissent) to the writings of St Paul, St Augustine and St Thomas Aquinas. St Paul, in his discussion of marriage in 1 Corinthians 7 does not make the Platonic link between marital ethics and procreation: there marriage is presented simply as a concession to the strength of sexual desire. The standard Christian teaching on sex and marriage, until recent centuries, was based on that of St Augustine – the only philosopher, among the Church Fathers and Latin scholastics, to have had personal experience of sex.

In modern times Augustine has acquired a reputation among non-Christians as a misogynist with a hatred of sex. Recent scholarship has shown that this reputation needs re-examination. Many fathers in the early Church taught that marriage was a consequence of the Fall, and that there would have been no sex in the Garden of Eden. Augustine maintained, on the contrary, that marriage was part of God's original plan for unfallen man and that Adam and Eve, even had they remained innocent, would have procreated by sexual union. Against ascetics who regarded virginity as the only decent option for a Christian, Augustine wrote a treatise defending marriage as a legitimate and honourable estate.

Augustine did indeed regard sex as permissible only in marriage and treated procreation as the principal purpose of marriage. Consequently he set limits on the types of sexual activity lawful between husband and wife. Husband and wife must not take any steps to prevent conception. Husband and wife must honour each other's reasonable requests for sexual intercourse, unless the request is for something unnatural. Since procreation is the divine purpose for sex, it goes almost without saying that only heterosexual intercourse is permissible.

Shameful acts against nature, like those of the
Sodomites, are to be detested and punished in
every place and every time. Even if all peoples
should do them, they would still incur the same
guilt by divine law, which did not make human
beings to use each other in that way. (*Confessions*,
3, 8, 15)

But the desire to procreate, Augustine concedes, is not
the only legitimate motive for marriage. Christians may
enter into it also to enjoy the special companionship
that links husband and wife. Once the need for procreation has been satisfied, husbands and wives, Augustine
thought, do well to refrain from intercourse and limit
themselves to continent companionship; but he did not
condemn intercourse after child-bearing age as sinful.
The strict link between copulation and procreation,
therefore, is absent even in Augustinian morality.

Moreover, Augustine thought that in assessing sexual
morality it is reasonable to take into account considerations about the optimum size of the overall population. In urging that lifelong celibacy, though not
obligatory, is a higher state than matrimony he makes
much of the point that there is no longer a need to
expand the human race – as there was in the days of the
polygamous Hebrew patriarchs.

When we turn from Augustine to Aquinas we find
that his teaching on the relations between the sexes is

139

much conditioned by the biological beliefs that he took over from Aristotle. For much of his life he believed that in biological generation the female merely provided nutrition for an active principle provided by the male. Since like begets like, a female is, on this view, an anomalous or defective male. Aquinas combined this theory of the transmission of human nature with the biblical account of the creation of the first pair to provide a basis for the subordination of women in medieval Christian society.

In our own time there are two dominant contrasting patterns of sexual morality.

Christian fundamentalists, not only in the Catholic Church, define a large number of sexual activities as intrinsically sinful. In my view it is wrong to regard sexual ethics as a matter of laying down rules concerning which kinds of sex are permissible in the way that one can specify the positions and motions of a bowler which will make a delivery a no-ball in cricket. In this as in other areas, the appropriate approach is not via the notion of law, but via the notion of virtue: in this case the virtue of chastity.

I do not wish to say that there are no such things as wrong sexual acts: of course there are. I agree with Aristotle that there can be no such thing as the right time and place and person for the commission of adultery. But adultery is wrong, not because it is a particular kind of sexual activity – most adulteries are sexual acts of a banal and normal kind – but because it is a breach of contract, a violation of fidelity towards one to whom one has promised exclusive sexual love. More obviously, rape is one of the worst of human acts, because it is a violation of the sexual integrity of an unconsenting partner.

At the opposite extreme from fundamentalism is the common secular position that everything is permitted in sex, whether solitary, or between partners of either gender or any species. The only moral constraint on sexual activity, according to this view, is the consent of any partner that may be involved. For this reason, the one form of sex that is universally abhorred is paedophilia, where the sexual partner is, by reason of age, incapable of the appropriate informed consent.

The permissive attitude to sex finds expression in the affirmation of a right to privacy. It is surely reasonable to accept that everyone has a right to a private life; but 'private life' has become more and more synonymous with 'sexual life'. The concept of privacy is a slippery one, and the right to privacy can be interpreted in several ways. Sex is private in the sense that commonly there are not, and normally there should not be, spectators of what goes on in the bedroom. Again, there is normally no good reason why the press or the police should interest themselves in discovering and documenting individuals' sexual history. But it is not at all true that sex of its nature is private in the sense of having no consequences for people other than the con-senting partners.

Often the privacy of sex seems to be taken to mean that any criticism of others' sexual behaviour is not only impolite and politically incorrect but positively immoral. The individual's sexual preferences are taken to override all considerations of the feelings and rights of others, whether spouses, children or colleagues. This is surely an untenable position, and it is unsurprising that in recent years there appears to have been a reaction against this attitude which goes beyond per-missiveness to the positive privileging of sex.

A rational sexual ethic, I would maintain, lies in the mean between the regulatory code of the puritan and the free-for-all of the libertine. What should be the guiding principle of morality in this area? I have already accepted that it is not possible to determine sexual ethics by closely linking sexual activity to its procre-ative potential. The division of sexual acts into natural and unnatural was undermined long ago by nature itself when, month by month, it separated human sexual desire from human fertility, and marked out humankind from the other animals who mate only when the female is on heat.

It is wrong, however, to forget altogether the biolog-ical function of sex. Moralists have always drawn para-llels between the ethics of sex and the ethics of food and drink. Traditionally, both instincts were the field of operation of the virtue of temperance. Nowadays the moral evaluation of eating behaviour is more closely linked to its biological efficiency than ever it was in the past: the consumption of fattening or otherwise unhealthy foods attracts instant censure. Contrariwise, the moral disapproval that once attached to sexual activity that did not contribute to the propagation of the race seems in our time to have evaporated. It is almost as if temperance was a corset which must be tightened at one point if it is to be let out at another.

The part of temperance that concerns sex was traditionally named chastity; and I would maintain that within the contemporary social and technological context chastity is best understood as the maintenance of the link, not between sex and procreation, but between sex and love. Because love is the most profound of human values, and sex is the most intense of human pleasures, it is important that the two should wherever possible go hand in hand. Promiscuity is bad not only because of the dangers it presents of unwanted pregnancies and sexually transmitted diseases, but because it devalues sex by separating it from love. Whether the partners in a sexual union love or try to love each other is more important than whether they are of the same or different sex. Experience shows that there may be much deeper love in a homosexual union than in many heterosexual marriages.

However, the contemporary distinction between homosexuals, heterosexuals and bisexuals does not seem to me to be helpful. There is, of course, no difficulty in discerning whether a particular sexual act is homoerotic or not. But other societies – notably ancient Greece – regarded an orientation towards homosexual union not as a lifetime characteristic of individuals, but as a phase likely to occur at a particular time in a single person's life. The moral discrimination to which they attached most importance was not that between heterosexual and homosexual activity but between active and passive homosexuality.

A more important distinction is surely that between innate and acquired sexual orientation, though there seems to be little agreement about the proportion of cases in which homosexual orientation is an unavoidable condition and those in which it is a freely chosen alternative lifestyle. A person who is incapable of enjoying heterosexual activity suffers a double disability: he or she is incapable of combining sexual pleasure with procreative function, and he or she is deprived of the possibility of combining intimate personal union with the diversity of experience distinguishing the different sexes. To be sure, many people are happy to forgo these advantages in favour of same-sex delight and same-sex love. Even if it is correct to regard an inborn homosexuality as a handicap – which many homosexuals would vehemently deny – that provides no reason for condemning, still less criminalizing, homosexual activity. As a homosexual friend put it to me, in the case of those who are unambiguously handicapped, such as those who lack hands, we encourage, rather than forbid or censure, their pursuit, by other parts of their body, of creative activities like writing and painting. One of the cruellest forms human folly has ever taken was the centuries-long practice of imprisoning, not to say burning, those convicted of sodomy.

Because an incapacity for normal heterosexual congress is, for the reasons given, a disability, I believe that any homosexual proselytizing, or the creation of a homosexual culture, is not to be encouraged. Nor do I welcome proposals for homosexual marriage. However much its original purpose has been downgraded in contemporary culture, marriage still remains an institution whose primary purpose is to provide a stable context for the procreation and education of children. Though I am myself the product of a single parent family, I have not been able to find evidence that children brought up in such households, or within single-sex unions, are likely to turn out just as well as those brought up within a happy marriage.

As I argued earlier in connection with adultery, the morality of marriage and its violations should be separated from the issue of chastity in sexual behaviour. Because I think that love, rather than procreation, is the crucial issue in the regulation of sex, I am happy for all the advantages – in respect of esteem, taxation, inheritance – which a spouse can confer on another spouse to be available in law to the partners in a homosexual union. But that is a different matter from treating homosexual union as indistinguishable from traditional marriage.

13

Happiness

For many ages, philosophers have discussed the nature of happiness. Some have placed the concept at the apex of their system of moral philosophy. Aristotle and Bentham, for instance, agreed in so doing, though they had very different conceptions of what happiness consisted in. Bentham equated happiness with pleasure, conceived as a warm feeling inside; Aristotle made a contrast between bodily pleasure and true happiness, whose highest expression was intellectual contemplation. But for both these philosophers happiness was a supreme good, which supplied the purpose, and measured the value, of human acting and striving.

Happiness has also been a cardinal notion in religious thought. Jesus' Sermon on the Mount, one of the founding texts of Christianity, begins with the eight 'beatitudes' which proclaim eight keys to blessedness or happiness. The first three, in the Jerusalem Bible, read as follows:

> How happy are the poor in spirit;
> Theirs is the kingdom of heaven.
> Happy the gentle;
> They shall have the earth for their heritage
> Happy those who mourn;
> They shall be comforted.
>
> (Mt. 5, 3–5)

St Augustine, in his book *On the Trinity* tells the story of a stage comedian who promised to tell his audience, at his next appearance, what was in each of their minds. When they returned he told them 'Each of you wants to buy cheap and sell dear'. This was smart, Augustine says, but not really correct – and he gives a list of possible counterexamples. But if the actor had said 'Each of you wants to be happy, and none of you wants to be miserable' then, Augustine says, he would have hit the mark perfectly.

Of course, not all religions are happiness-oriented in this way. Happiness, however differently it may be defined, seems essentially to involve the satisfaction of one's wants; and in Buddhism release from the sufferings of life is to be sought through the suppression, not the satisfaction, of desire. And the happiness promised to religious people may be placed in the world as we know it (as in much of the Hebrew Bible) or in some future state which is yet to be made manifest (as in Islam and Christianity). The old Catholic Catechism, in response to the question 'Why did God make you?', answered 'God made me to know him, love him, and serve him in this world, and to be happy with him for ever *in the next*'.

In recent years not only philosophers and theologians, but highly worldly people such as economists have been taking an interest in the nature of happiness. Of course, ever since Bentham and Mill founded the philosophy of utilitarianism, economists have been keenly interested in the maximizing of utility, which for Bentham was identical with pleasure and with happiness. But utility, while an overarching economic concept, has until recently remained a largely unexamined one. Utility has been regarded simply as whatever it is that indifference curves measure.

But even economists are coming to realize that the development of the economy is after all only a means to an end: economic performance matters only in so far as it makes people happier. So economists have begun to take an interest in discovering independent measures of happiness to find out to what extent economic growth promotes happiness. As a first step to finding this out, economists have taken to asking people whether or not they feel happy.

The answers to the questionnaires have produced some interesting results. The great increases in average income in the developed economies during recent decades do not seem to have been accompanied by any similar increase in the percentage of people willing to describe themselves as happy or very happy. A certain level of well-being seems to be, for most people, a necessary condition for happiness, but it is far from being sufficient. Once a certain standard of living has been secured, there seems to be no further correlation between economic growth and self-reported happiness.

We may perhaps wonder whether self-reporting is an appropriate way of measuring happiness. It is widely agreed that there are problems in comparing self-ascriptions in different countries and cultures: there are subtle differences between the meaning of words like 'happiness', 'contentment' and 'satisfaction' in English and between their near-synonyms in other languages. But there is a more fundamental question that transcends local linguistic differences. Is it really true that individuals are the best authorities on their own happiness? Do I necessarily know whether I am really happy?

The answer to these questions depends on one's underlying conception of happiness. For Bentham and those who think of happiness as a warm feeling the answer is obviously yes. Pleasure and pain are opposites, and it is as natural to take an interviewee's word for it that she is very happy as it is to take a patient's word for it that he is in great pain. According to Plato and Aristotle, however, most people are ignorant of the true nature of happiness and therefore do not really know whether they are happy or not. Many people, Aristotle said, equate happiness with the enjoyment of sensual pleasure or the possession of political power, or the combination of the two in the life of an Oriental despot. In reality, Aristotle believed, the stable and rewarding satisfaction that we all seek is only to be found in the exercise of human virtue, in particular the virtues of the intellect. But this key to the nature of happiness is a secret known only to few.

Of course, Aristotle wrote in Greek not in English, and it might be suggested that his distance from the utilitarian conception of happiness simply shows that 'happiness' is not a good translation of his Greek word '*eudaimonia*'. But this would be too simple. Both Aristotle and Bentham are employing the same fundamental concept of a supreme value that provides the motivation and the measure for human activity. I shall try to identify the elements of this concept, which has a role in many different philosophical systems and many different historic cultures, however it may be expressed in the idiom of different languages. To circumvent linguistic difficulties with the word 'happiness' I shall speak henceforth of 'well-being'.

In the concept of human well-being, I shall argue, there are three distinct elements. I shall call them contentment, welfare and dignity.

Contentment is what is measured by self-ascriptions of happiness. It is not so much a feeling or sensation as an attitude or state of mind; but of the elements of well-being it is the one which is closest to the utilitarian idea of happiness. If contentment is to amount to a constituent of well-being it must be an enduring and stable state; not mere temporary euphoria or glow of satisfaction.

Welfare consists in the satisfaction of one's animal needs, for food, drink, shelter and the other things that conduce to bodily flourishing. Self-ascription does not have the same central role in the measurement of welfare as it does in the case of contentment; we may be mistaken about the state of our bodily health, and other people are often better placed to make a judgement here.

Dignity is a more complicated notion to define, but we may say initially that it involves the control of one's own destiny and the ability to live a life of one's choice. Because one's dignity concerns, among other things, one's relationship to other people, there cannot be absolute and objective measurements of dignity as there can of welfare.

These three elements vary independently. Each of them may exist without the others; and more importantly, pairs of the triad may occur without the third.

It is possible for someone to have welfare and contentment without dignity. A well-housed and well-fed slave, who looks for nothing better than his servile lot and has no complaints about the way he is treated, may be thought of as being in a certain sense quite happy.

Contentment and dignity may be present without welfare. A devout and ascetic hermit, revered by all who come in contact with him, may regard himself as blessed even though he may be undernourished and unhealthy. If we look for a secular example, we may think of hunger strikers, admired by a throng of supporters, suffering resolutely to further a cause they believe to be paramount. Both religious and secular martyrs have died proclaiming their happiness.

It is easy, too, for welfare and dignity to be present without contentment, as in the case of a bored and pampered member of a rich and dominant elite.

Many of the problems and paradoxes that have perplexed those who have sought to understand the nature of happiness are removed if we resolve it into these separate elements. Let us look closer at each of them in turn.

Contentment is a necessary but not a sufficient condition of well-being. If people are contented with their lot, that does not necessarily mean that their lot is a happy lot. Their contentment may derive from ignorance, or from a false evaluation of alternatives, or from a lack of imagination. We might call such contentment the contentment of the unraised consciousness. In less contemporary idiom we might call it the contentment of the unexamined life, which Socrates thought was not worth living. You may think you are well off and yet not be; equally, you can be well off and not know it. In either case, something is lacking to your well-being.

It is the presence or absence of contentment, rather than of welfare or dignity, which is measured by the responses of those that are the subjects of questionnaires on happiness. Even as a measure of contentment, responses to questionnaires are problematic. Self-ascription may lack sincerity: a person may be too proud to reveal discontent, or too superstitious to boast of happiness. One may belong to a culture, or occupy a status, which is hostile to whingeing or fearful of hubris. Again, self-ascription may lack stability: the euphoric state of mind candidly avowed to the questioner may turn out to be no more than a passing mood. So too may be the depression which leads one to place oneself into the lowest of the questioner's response bands.

We are not necessarily good at predicting our own future contentment. King Midas thought that he would be happy if he could turn everything into gold at a touch. As his case shows dramatically, the satisfaction of our wishes does not always lead to contentment. St Teresa once said that more tears were shed over prayers that had been answered than over prayers which had not been granted.

Despite all the problems, self-ascription does provide a rough and ready measure of contentment. Avowals, however, whether spontaneous or solicited by pollsters, are not the only expressions of contentment. Laughter, smiling, scowling, weeping, posture, comportment and other behaviours give us an indication of others' content or discontent; so too the style and energy of their application to their daily tasks. Such behavioural indications provide, to some extent, an objective check on the sincerity of linguistic expressions of subjective contentment. Psychologists, too, claim to have discovered chemical features of the brain which are found empirically to correlate with the verbal and behavioural criteria of contentment. However, contentment is only a single element in well-being.

Of course, contentment is a valuable thing, and for individuals in many circumstances it may be wisest to aim at nothing more: the other elements of well-being may be, through no fault of their own, outside their reach. If I am going to remain poor and powerless for the rest of my life, I had best count whatever blessings I have. I do well to trim my desires to those that can be satisfied in practice. But if this is a reasonable attitude to take with regard to one's own life, it is surely an inadequate one for those responsible for the well-being of others. To the extent that we can we have to ensure not just that others are resigned to their narrow lot, but that they have appropriate options and wide horizons. 'They're perfectly happy as they are' is the slogan of the exploiter throughout the ages, whether it is masters exploiting slaves, or males exploiting females, or one racial group exploiting another.

I turn from contentment to welfare, the second of the three elements of well-being. Methodologically, welfare is the simplest of the three elements to identify and analyse. It is objective, it is easily measured and it is universally agreed to be a good and to be a component of well-being. Unambiguous measurements are possible of the caloric intake of individuals, the expectation of life of particular groups and other parameters constitutive of welfare. Each of us recognizes that medical check-ups may be a more reliable guide to the good or ill condition of our body than any subjective feeling of illness or well-being.

The third element in well-being, which I have labelled 'dignity' is both more complex and more contentious to analyse. It is related to welfare in the following way: a fundamental element of human dignity is the individual's awareness of his or her absolute and relative position with regard to welfare. Deliberately to keep people in ignorance of this is an affront to their dignity, even if it may increase their contentment. To balance dignity against contentment is a crucial and difficult task for those with responsibility for other people's welfare – nowhere more obviously than when we are considering the situation of the terminally ill.

Over and above this basic awareness of one's status in terms of welfare, dignity has three elements, which we may refer to in shorthand as choice, value and prestige. To possess dignity you must have a degree of choice and control over your life, the life that you lead must be a worthwhile one and it must carry with it a degree of prestige. These three elements are not all on the same level; but all of them must be investigated if we are to assess a person's well-being.

Even the most downtrodden of us is constantly faced with choices in daily life; but obviously not all choices are significant. The freedom to choose between blue cheese and thousand-island dressing on one's salad is not a valuable component of liberty or dignity. Three most important choices are the choice of one's cultural identity, the choice of one's social role and the choice of the political arrangements under which one lives.

It is an important part of dignity that key elements of one's cultural identity, such as one's religion or one's language, are not forced upon one unwillingly from outside. The choice of cultural identity is obviously very largely a matter of *consent*. We are brought up as part of an ethnic group, with a certain language, customs, morality and religion; we cannot decide in advance what is to be the culture into which we are born and educated. What matters is that when we come of age to take responsibility for ourselves we should willingly identify with that culture, or be able, if we do not, to alter or discard features of it, or to adopt a different one.

When it is not our cultural identity, but our social role, that is to be defined, then it is an element of dignity that choice, and not mere consent, should enter

157

in. For this reason, there is greater dignity in marriage to a partner of one's choice than in a marriage arranged by one's family and friends. This is so, whether or not an arranged marriage may lead in certain cases to securer welfare and greater contentment. Again, there is greater dignity in working at a job that one has freely contracted to perform than in carrying out duties which are assigned one willy-nilly by one's social status.

A third, but in my view less important, constituent of the control of one's life which is an element in dignity is one's degree of participation in the political arrangements under which one lives. A person who has control over the rulers who govern him to the extent that he can help to vote them out in a future election clearly enjoys greater political choice than one who has no such control.

We have identified three elements of the control over one's life which is one of the constituents of dignity. But such control, though necessary, is not a sufficient condition of the kind of dignity that I am talking about. For a life may be totally under one's control, and yet undeserving of respect because dissipated in pointless activities. For the dignity which is of the essence of well-being a life must involve activities which are worthwhile in themselves and not mere devices to pass the time.

In deciding whether activities are worthwhile there are subjective and objective factors to take into account. Whether a particular type of work confers dignity depends both on the degree of job-satisfaction of the person employed, and on the value placed on it by society. Obviously, many very different types of job may provide satisfaction and esteem: but it is an essential element of well-being that the manner in which one provides for the welfare of oneself and one's dependents should not be mere drudgery. Of course, not only work but also leisure falls to be assessed on the scale of dignity, as it ranges from the creativity of an artist to the torpidity of a couch potato. Some philosophers indeed, of an aristocratic bent, have thought that only leisure activities could confer dignity: paid work was of its very nature degrading. In our own time it is unemployment, rather than employment, that is an affront to one's dignity.

In addition to choice and worthwhile activity the third element which I identified in dignity is prestige. Prestige is not, as the other elements of dignity are, an essential constituent of well-being; but it can undoubtedly contribute to it and augment it. Prestige is based on one's possession of goods of a kind which arouse the respect and envy of others. Such goods need not be material goods, but they are bound to be positional goods: goods which relate to one's position in society and of their nature cannot be universally shared, since, in the words of W. S. Gilbert, when everyone is somebody, then nobody's anybody.

Dignity, as I have defined it, is not at all restricted to people occupying positions of wealth and power in economically advanced societies. St Simeon Stylites, a hermit who spent his life in prayer at the top of a pillar, revered by pilgrims who flocked to assist in his devotions, was a man who lived a life of his choice, in an activity which he and his society regarded as the most worthwhile of all activities, and who enjoyed the esteem of all his contemporaries. He possessed each of the three elements of the dignity which is a constituent of well-being.

I have now broken down the notion of well-being into three independent items, contentment, welfare and dignity, and analysed each of these in turn. My aim was not to show that no one could be happy who did not score highly on each of these parameters. Throughout history, few have been fortunate enough to be in possession of all the desirable characteristics we have identified. The purpose of the analysis was rather to show that when we pursue happiness for ourselves or others the goal is not a simple but a complex one, and that if we are trying to measure happiness a single metric will not suffice. Policies for the maximization of well-being may well involve trade-offs between dignity and contentment, between welfare and dignity and between contentment and welfare.

The answer to the question to what extent does economic development promote well-being appears reasonably clear now that we have separated out the different ingredients of well-being. Development assists contentment to the extent that it assists welfare. Once a certain level of per capita income has been reached in a country, further growth appears not to lead to further contentment. However, even in rich countries development can help dignity by removing drudgery. The provision of washing machines and dishwashers has given possibilities for fuller lives to those doing housework even in the richest of countries. While resignation may be a virtue, it can be exercised in nobler contexts than in that of washing dishes. But of course, affluent householders in the developed nations have much less to complain of than the breadwinners of the Third World, and the fact that domestic appliances can make a genuine contribution to their well-being does not mean that their provision should have priority over the satisfaction of the basic welfare needs of the poor.

Besides the economic question, there is a political question. Does democracy promote happiness? Here again, we have to distinguish between the different elements of well-being. I have suggested above that a degree of control over the way in which one is governed is a factor which contributes to one's dignity; and therefore, to the extent to which dignity is a crucial element in well-being, some form of democracy is not just a cause but a constituent of well-being. But the more interesting inquiry is whether democracy is a positive causal factor in the production of welfare and contentment.

To answer this question we must once again make distinctions, but this time in relation not to the concept of happiness but to the concept of democracy. There are several separable features which make up the democratic institutions which are prized in first world countries. Most important are the basic human rights of freedom from torture and degrading treatment by government: without these rights welfare, dignity and contentment are all under threat. But there are other important features of political arrangements which are less immediately connected with the elements of well-being. One is the citizens' ability to choose and change governments by elections. Another is the independence of incorrupt courts. Another is the existence of an effectively functioning market.

Recent history suggests that a market operating in comparative freedom is the most effective agent for the production of national wealth. Since there is undoubtedly a strong link between wealth and health, which is the core of welfare, the freedom of the market can claim to be an important causal factor in the generation of that element of well-being. And an effective market depends on effective government to maintain civil order and impartial courts to enforce commercial contracts. Hence the preference for capitalist democracy among economists concerned to promote well-being.

While the free-market economy may be the most efficient tool so far discovered to provide the means of welfare, it does not necessarily follow that it maximizes contentment. There are several reasons for this. In the first place, once basic needs have been satisfied, many people are more concerned with dignity than welfare, and the operation of the market may diminish, rather than increase, the dignity of those engaged in it. Members of traditionally dignified professions may feel insulted if their services are rated simply at market value. The great inequalities which the free operation of the market allows to build up may cause great discontent among those at the lower end of the scale, even if in absolute terms their income is large enough to provide them with adequate welfare. Unlike some other philosophers, I do not myself regard inequality of wealth as being in and of itself an affront to human dignity. For my part, I do not count myself as at all degraded simply because some other people are very much richer than I am. If the existence of billionaires is the price to be paid for an economic system which is the most efficient method of generating wealth for all of us, then it is a price I am willing to pay. What matters in judging the merits of societies and economic systems is not the spread of incomes, but the absolute level of those worst off. Of course, those with great wealth may use their economic power to bring other people into a condition where their welfare and dignity is genuinely compromised. They may also be seriously at fault by not using their wealth to improve the lot of the poorest. But heartlessness and exploitation are not necessary concomitants of riches.

I have been fortunate to have had a very happy life, based on a happy marriage, and with a career in which there was never any clear boundary between work and pleasure. Unlike many of my friends, I do not look forward to any afterlife. If one is a Cartesian philosopher and regards the soul as a self-standing entity temporarily and contingently linked to a body, then one may consistently believe in immortality. But I reject Cartesianism and think that I am a mortal rational animal. My mental life is so bound up with the movements and behaviour of my body – my eyes, tongue, lips, hands and so on – that I find it inconceivable that it can survive the death of that body. Christian tradition has held out hope of an eventual universal resurrection: but a body resembling mine a millennium hence would not be my body. Unless one believes in the possibility of a disembodied soul in the interim, there is nothing to link that resurrection body with the mortal one in which I now live. Descriptions of the condition of resurrected bodies (which are rarely offered by modern Christians, but which are amply provided by Augustine and Aquinas) make them appear not only to be unidentifiable with particular mundane individuals, but even to belong to some species quite different from the human race.

Some people are disturbed by the thought that at their death they will be annihilated. For myself I find it no more disconcerting to accept that in the future the world will continue in my absence than to accept that for millions of years previously it got on very well without me. It is rather the possibility of continuing after death that I find troubling. It is not just that annihilation would be vastly preferable to the torments of the damned so lovingly described by Dante; it is that even painless perpetuity would be appalling.

The point was well made by John Stuart Mill in *Essays on Theism* (1889). While admitting that in the appalling conditions of early-nineteenth-century England the only hope of happiness that many had was to imagine it in another life, he went on

It is not only possible but probable that in a higher, and above all, a happier condition of human life, not annihilation but immortality may be the burdensome idea; and that human nature, though pleased with the present, and by no means impatient to quit it, would find comfort and not sadness in the thought that it is not chained through eternity to a conscious existence which it cannot be assured that it will always wish to preserve. (p. 122)

Bibliographical Note

In this short book many statements are made dogmatically without proof or supporting evidence. On most of the topics covered I have written at greater length elsewhere. Those who are interested may find the themes and arguments of the different chapters developed in the books listed below.

1. I have written two volumes of autobiography: *A Path from Rome* (Oxford, 1985) and *A Life in Oxford* (John Murray, 1997).
2. The nature of philosophy is discussed in my *Wittgenstein* (Penguin, 1973; Blackwell, 2006) and in *The Legacy of Wittgenstein* (Blackwell, 1984).
3, 4 and 5. Arguments for and against theism are presented and criticized in *The Five Ways* (Routledge, 1969, 2002), *The God of the Philosophers* (Oxford, 1979) and *The Unknown God* (Continuum, 2004).
6. *Reason and Religion* (Blackwell, 1987) and *What is Faith?* (Oxford, 1992) deal *inter alia* with issues raised here.

7. *The Metaphysics of Mind* (Oxford, 1989) gives a full exposition of the philosophical anthropology here sketched.

8. The historical material in this chapter is presented more fully in *A Brief History of Western Philosophy* (Blackwell, 1998).

9. I presented some of the substance of this chapter in a review of David Albert Jones' *The Soul of the Embryo* (Continuum, 2004), a book to which I am indebted for much of the factual information here presented.

10. The key argument of this chapter I first set out in *The Development of Mind* (Edinburgh University Press, 1973).

11. The theory of the just war is treated at length in my *The Logic of Deterrence* (Firethorn, 1985).

12. The history of sexual ethics is a topic included in the two volumes that have so far appeared of my *New History of Western Philosophy* (Oxford, 2004).

13. I have treated of happiness in *Aristotle on the Perfect Life* (Oxford, 1992).

Index

169

INDEX

INDEX

INDEX